7

The Development of
SEGREGATIONIST
THOUGHT

THE DORSEY SERIES IN AMERICAN HISTORY

Editor *IRVIN G. WYLLIE* *University of Wisconsin, Parkside Campus*

Sale & Karn *American Expansion: A Book of Maps*

Glaab *The American City: A Documentary History*

Quint, Albertson, & Cantor *Main Problems in American History*

Cronon *Twentieth Century America: Selected Readings*

Van Tassel & Hall *Science and Society in the United States*

Crowe *The Age of Civil War and Reconstruction, 1830-1900: A Book of Interpretative Essays*

Wilson *Darwinism and the American Intellectual: A Book of Readings*

Cole *An Interpretive History of American Foreign Relations*

Kaplan *Recent American Foreign Policy: Conflicting Interpretations*

Filene *American Views of Soviet Russia, 1917-1965*

Newby *The Development of Segregationist Thought*

The Development of
SEGREGATIONIST
THOUGHT

Edited by

I. A. NEWBY

California State College
Fullerton, California

1968

THE DORSEY PRESS   Homewood, Illinois

IRWIN-DORSEY LIMITED   Nobleton, Ontario

First Printing, May, 1968
Second Printing, January, 1969

Library of Congress Catalog Card No. 68-23348

Printed in the United States of America

Foreword

The study of anti-Negro racism is difficult and disagreeable—and necessary. The subject itself is complex and multifaceted; the literature of segregation and white supremacy is voluminous and diverse. All of this compounds the difficulties of compiling a representative anthology of segregationist writings. I selected the items in this collection with two purposes in mind: (1) to illustrate the major ideas of segregationist thought since 1890, and (2) to demonstrate significant features of the white supremacy mentality. Of course no collection as brief as this one is entirely satisfactory. I hope, however, that the materials reprinted here will give the reader some understanding of the nature, intensity, and tenacity of anti-Negro ideas in America.

These materials make painful reading. One's initial impulse is to forget them, especially since they now have so little scientific and scholarly authority. But to ignore a disagreeable subject is not to be rid of it. Dedicated segregationists still accept the ideas of anti-Negro racism, and to study those ideas is to remind ourselves of the most sensitive and distressing episode in our history, the degradation of Negro Americans. Segregationist thought is thus an essential element in the most persistent problem in American history—race relations, or more precisely, the chronic controversy over the Negro's place in American life. It should not be ignored.

Negroes have not yet achieved equality in America. To understand why this is so is one of the imperatives of American citizenship today. I believe in the final analysis it is the result of white attitudes toward Negroes—and the actions those attitudes have inspired. Negroes never achieved equality because whites never permitted it. Controlling the instruments of power, prestige, and status, whites united to keep Negroes impoverished, uneducated, disfranchised, degraded, dependent—and brainwashed. In their view these were the natural conditions of Negroes. What whites have believed about Negroes and why they believed it, what they have done to the race in America and why they did it—these are questions which the study of segregationist thought can illuminate.

I have not felt it necessary to challenge every error or distortion in the items reprinted in this collection. A general rebuttal is contained in the Epilogue. The footnotes to the selections reprinted are intended to clarify particular references or elucidate specific points made by the authors. A Bibliographical Essay at the end contains suggestions for further reading on both sides of the subject.

Fullerton, California   I. A. Newby
April, 1968

Table of Contents

Introduction: Segregationist Thought since 1890

Over the last generation Americans have become increasingly aware of race and the historical roots of contemporary racial problems. There is a new interest in Negro history, greater appreciation of Negro contributions to the national heritage, more sympathy for men and movements who champion the cause of Negroes and labor for racial equality and interracial cooperation. A new dimension in the history of race relations has emerged as historians have pushed the roots of the Negro rights movement further and further into the past.

All this should be applauded. Its net result is a new perspective in the history of race relations which was long overdue in coming. Our sudden concern for Negroes and equalitarians is legitimate, but in recovering their history we must keep a proper perspective. Anti-Negro groups of various names—racists, segregationists, white supremacists—have almost always controlled race relations in this country and have therefore defined the role of Negroes in American life. This fact must not be forgotten; to do so would be to risk distortion of the record we are ourselves trying to correct. Current racial problems have deep historical roots; Negro Americans today are products of a historical experience markedly different from that of whites. To understand those problems and the Negro's plight today, we must know (and keep in mind) the role of anti-Negro groups in the history of race relations in America. This means, among other things, that we must understand anti-Negro thought, that is, the body of ideas and attitudes centering around belief in racial inequality and Negro inferiority.

This is not an easy task. In studying any subject relating to race there is a temptation, indeed a tendency, to dismiss those who disagree with our own views as nothing more than prejudiced bigots. Such epithets may be apt descriptions of many segregationists, but name-calling is a poor substitute for careful study. The first task of equalitarians is to understand the racist; only then can they effectively combat racist policies. In the final analysis, one's attitude toward

1

race and related subjects rests upon initial assumptions and value judgments concerning such debatable things as human nature, heredity and environment, the relationship of the individual to society, the nature of American democracy, the meaning of race itself. To say that an individual is prejudiced is to say, in part at least, that his assumptions concerning these subjects differ from one's own. Racists believe that race is the transcendent fact of life; that human nature is fixed by heredity and immune to environment and therefore related to race; that intelligence and behavior are genetically determined and also related to race; that races differ fundamentally and the differences are relevant to public policy. The disagreement between racists and equalitarians thus involves a conflict of initial assumptions and rival value systems, and cannot be resolved to everyone's satisfaction by appeals to authority or objective data. In the social sciences, authorities mean different things to different men; "the facts" are subject to varying interpretations even by well-meaning men. There are data which *may* be interpreted as evidence of racial inequality; other data, however, seem clearly to indicate that races are approximately equal, or potentially so.

This does not mean the issue is purely relative. The evidence amassed by equalitarians is vastly superior to that of racists. Nor does it mean segregationists would be correct in their public policies even if their data were valid. In formulating public policy in a democracy, political and constitutional considerations are more important than raw scientific and historical data. What it does mean is that men have difficulty studying race. Rare indeed is the individual who changes his racial views as a result of scholarly inquiry. In the last half century scores of psychologists, some racists and others equalitarians, have studied the relative intelligence of whites and Negroes. As far as I know, not one of them ever drew conclusions from a specific study which were not implicit in the racial views he had before making the study. Racists invariably found support for their racism, and just as invariably equalitarians found evidence to strengthen their equalitarianism.

The purpose of this Introduction is to attempt, in spite of these hazards, to characterize segregationist thought since 1890; the selections which make up the body of this collection are intended to illustrate the major ideas of the segregationist argument. Hopefully, the work as a whole will illuminate the segregationist mind. Anti-Negro ideas have undergone a distinct evolution since 1890, yet the purpose behind those ideas has remained remarkably consistent. That purpose has been to define the proper place for Negroes in American life, proper, that is, in the eyes of segregationists and white supremacists. Segregationist thought has thus been designed to justify the treatment of Negroes in America (and especially in the South). It is therefore a rationalization for social segregation, educational discrimination, political subordination, and economic exploitation. It served the dual purpose of reassuring southern whites of the rightness of their racial policies and securing the acquiescence of other whites in those policies. It was broad enough and imprecise enough to appeal to whites of diverse racial views—extremists and moderates, reformers and conservatives, patricians and poor whites. By picking and choosing among its many facets, men of distinctly different, even contradictory, racial views could find authority for their positions.

To commence the study of segregationist thought in 1890 is somewhat artificial. Like most chronological divisions of historical subjects, this one is open to some criticism. Eighteen-ninety saw no sharp change in the development of anti-Negro ideas; it is, however, a convenient date to mark the beginning of a new era in race relations in the South and the nation as a whole. The Mississippi Constitutional Convention of that year commenced the long, dreary process by which southern states disfranchised their Negro citizens, relegated them to a segregated, second-class status, and constructed a legal, constitutional defense for those new policies. The defeat of Senator Henry Cabot Lodge's Force bill in the same year marked the last concerted effort in Congress to challenge disfranchisement and segregation. Booker T. Washington's Atlanta Exposition Address of 1895 was taken by whites to mean that Negroes accepted segregation. The *Plessy* v. *Ferguson* decision of 1896 in effect wrote racial segregation into the constitutional law of the land. The new era in race relations was accompanied by changes in the racial attitudes of white Americans, and the result was a flood of literature explaining and defending the new racial policies. The racial views expounded in that literature constitute the core of segregationist thought in the 20th century.

Three distinct though overlapping periods are discernible in the evolution of segregationist ideas since 1890: (1) from 1890 to the 1920's, (2) from the 1920's to 1954, (3) since 1954. During the first (and most important) of these periods, the basic ideas of segregationists crystallized, received systematic and authoritative exposition, and enjoyed widespread respectability in academic and intellectual circles. Anti-Negro racism was the fashion of the day, as white America busied itself defining and implementing the new status of Negro Americans.

In the generation after 1890 the biological sciences, the new social sciences, history, and the Bible were the principal sources of authority for anti-Negro ideas. Segregationists with an intellectual bent, that is, those most interested in systematically developing their ideas, found the biological and social sciences especially useful. Before the 1920's, opinion in those disciplines, as well as in history, generally accepted (or failed to challenge) the idea of racial inequality and Negro inferiority. It is a chastening fact that the advances made in those disciplines in the generation before World War I enhanced rather than eroded the authority of racist ideas.

Segregationist thought in the early 20th century was thus an amalgam of science, social science, history, and religion. All segregationists were interested in proving that Negroes are inferior to Caucasians, for without such proof their racial policies were indefensible. Scientific racists, that is, those segregationists who sought this proof in science or social science, explained racial differences and inequalities as the result of evolutionary adaptations to differing environments. Negroes, they said, evolved in the lush jungles of tropical Africa where food was plentiful and shelter and clothing unnecessary. Nature made few demands upon the individual, and the race remained primitive. Caucasians, on the other hand, evolved in the frigid North where life was a constant challenge and only the clever and resourceful survived. Whites evolved upward into a superior race. During countless centuries of isolation each race intrabred and, free from the "alien" genes of other races, achieved genetic equilibrium in the individual and the race. Preserved and transmitted by heredity, this equilibrium is upset by racial interbreeding. Interbreeding—and intermarriage—are thus genetically harmful, and when practiced on a large scale will produce racial and national degeneration.

Physical and genetic differences between races, continued these racists, produce correspondingly significant differences in social behavior. Immorality, illegitimacy, broken families, unemployment, violence, irresponsibility, childishness—such conditions among Negroes, they insisted, are outward manifestations of innate racial qualities. Put another way, the Negro's position in America, whether social, economic, or political, is the inevitable consequence of his racial inadequacy. Because of inherent limitations, he cannot absorb

American civilization, the institutions of which are products of the white man's racial genius. Democracy, constitutionalism, Christianity, free enterprise, modern technology are beyond the Negro's racial capacity; he cannot compete in a society based upon them.

These ideas posited a direct correlation between race and civilization. Each race, so the thesis ran, creates its own civilization which reflects its unique racial genius. To the extent races differ in genius, so will the civilizations they create, and to that extent one cannot absorb the civilization of another. No civilization can survive an influx of racial aliens, if the aliens be given political equality or the right to intermarry. Mongrelization will destroy a civilization more thoroughly than conquering armies, for when mixed, racial characteristics, like water, seek the lowest possible level.

The usefulness of these ideas to white supremacists is obvious. Scientific racism, however, was more attractive and meaningful to race theorists than to the average southern segregationist. The latter was more interested in practical problems of racial policy than in systematic exposition of racial ideas. He was likely to be a Christian fundamentalist and biblical literalist and to suspect that scientific racism relied too much upon Darwinism and smacked of heresy or atheism. He therefore sought authority for his racial views in religion. Despite major differences, the parallels between scientific and religious racists were striking. Both sought unchallengeable authority for Negro inferiority and racial segregation. One found it in science, the other in the Bible and Christian principles (as they interpreted those principles). Both were concerned with ultimate causation, though this was less a problem for religious racists. They merely recognized racial inequality as self-evident and accepted it as God's will. One of them summarized the basic ideas of religious racism this way:

If God Almighty had intended the two races to be equal, He would have so created them. He made the Caucasian of handsome figure, straight hair, regular features, high brow, and superior intellect. He created the negro, giving him a black skin, kinky hair, thick lips, flat nose, low brow, low order of intelligence, and repulsive features. I do not believe that these differences were the result of either accident or mistake on the part of the Creator. I believe He knew what He was doing, and I believe He did just what He wanted to do.

Segregationists, as this view continued, "believe in God, and . . . are willing to accept His work just as it fell from His hands."

Integrationists, on the other hand "are quite sure that they can make a better job of it than did the Creator, hence we find them attempting to remove the black man from the menial sphere for which he was created, and where he may be useful, to a higher circle, for which he is entirely unfitted and where he is perfectly useless."[1]

Such was the religious racism of extremists and demagogues. Moderates, however, also made wide use of religion and gave it a different focus. Emphasizing the New Testament principles of love and charity, they saw Christianity as a bedrock upon which interracial cooperation and goodwill could be erected. The race problem will disappear from the South when both races learn "to think, feel and act right towards each other," wrote Robert Edwin Smith of Texas in 1922. "The question arises then," he continued, "what constitutes right thinking concerning the Negro race?" First, he wrote, "we must have open minds and honest purpose to begin with." Then, "we must strike out to the high hills from whence wisdom and understanding come and seek the mind and spirit of the Infinite One. 'If any man lacks wisdom, let him ask of God.' The mind of Christ must possess us, or we shall never think and see aright on any moral question." Surely, few of us would argue with Smith's generalities, or with his statement that "deep-rooted and age-long prejudices must give place to sincere purpose to discover the truth and then follow the truth wheresoever it may lead us." However, the implications of this for racial policy are unclear, or rather depend upon one's understanding of "the mind of Christ." Smith found nothing in his principles to cause difficulty for Christian segregationists. "Negroes must recognize the supremacy of the white race and be willing to be a good second," he declared. "Right-thinking white people will welcome all the progress and all the good that the race may achieve. But as conditions now stand, and as far as the future can be forecasted, the Caucasian race seems destined to lead all other races. Only the shifting of the now apparent purposes of the Supreme Arbiter of Nations will make it otherwise."[2]

History was the other basic element of segregationist thought. From it segregationists derived two of their most elemental beliefs: first, Negro Africa never produced a civilization worthy of the name

[1]U.S. *Cong. Record*, vol. 42, part 8, 60th Cong., 1st sess., February 22, 1908, Appendix, 40.

[2]Robert Edwin Smith, *Christianity and the Race Problem* (New York, 1922), pp. 121, 138.

and remained even yet a land of savagery and cannibalism; and second, the history of Negroes in America demonstrates the race's incapacity for responsible citizenship. In their effort to prove the latter, segregationists received substantial assistance from historians, many of whom believed explicitly in Negro inferiority. The views of James Ford Rhodes, one of the most distinguished historians of his generation, were not untypical. "Three and a half million persons of one of the most inferior races of mankind had through the agency of their superiors been transformed from slavery to freedom," wrote Rhodes in reference to Negroes at the end of the Civil War. "It was a race the children of which might with favouring circumstances show an intellectual development equal to white children 'up to the age of thirteen or fourteen; but then there comes a diminution often a cessation of their mental development. The physical overslaughs [sic] the psychical and they turn away from the pursuit of culture.' "[3]

Because such views were so widely shared by historians, American history, especially as written before the 1930's, conformed in important particulars to the needs of segregationists and designing racists. Historians told segregationists that slavery was a benevolence for Negroes, a humane and necessary instrument for transforming savages into useful, contented members of a Christian civilization. Negroes "have been the world's premium slaves," U. B. Phillips wrote in 1918 in *American Negro Slavery*,[4] and his work was still the standard authority on slavery when the *Brown* decision was issued in 1954. Historians told segregationists that abolitionists were fanatical busybodies bent upon destroying the Constitution and even the union itself, a characterization Allen Tate reflected in 1928 when he described abolitionists as "people in New England who wanted to destroy democracy and civil liberties in America by freeing the slaves."[5] This juxtaposing of slavery, democracy, and civil liberties is an illuminating insight into the anti-Negro mind.

Like segregationists, historians of the late 19th and early 20th centuries generally assigned base motives to racial reformers, but were sympathetic to advocates of racial repression and white supremacy. Invariably they thought the collapse of Radical Reconstruction a step in the right direction, and generally pictured disfranchisement as a

---

[3] James Ford Rhodes, *History of the United States* (New York, 1909), Vol. IV, p. 556.

[4] U. B. Phillips, *American Negro Slavery* (New York, 1918), p. 8.

[5] Allen Tate, *Stonewall Jackson, The Good Soldier* (New York, 1928), p. 25.

8

necessary reform. Indeed, historians were most helpful to segregationists in their descriptions of Radical Reconstruction. As James Ford Rhodes, William Archibald Dunning, and other scholars described Radical Reconstruction, it was little more than a "riot of Africanism," or in Claude Bowers' phrase, a "crusade of hate and social equality"—another juxtaposition which reveals much about racist thinking.[6] It was an episode which convincingly demonstrated what white supremacists were then saying—that Negroes are incapable of self-government and of exercising the responsibilities of American citizenship. Reading the historians' works one gets no inkling of the horrors of white supremacy, or the hopes and accomplishments of Negroes. When Negroes are not a problem for white men, they disappear entirely from the historians' accounts, leaving a distinct impression that the race made no worthwhile contribution to the nation's history.

The significance of the racism thus written into American history was enhanced by two things. The historians themselves had typically studied in the nation's best graduate schools, and they comprised the first generation of professional academic historians in America. Their history thus carried the authority of professional competence. In addition, they wrote while the South was undergoing a revolution in race relations, and white supremacists took their history of 19th-century America as proof of the necessity for disfranchisement and segregation. The white supremacists did not misread the historians. If the historians had been correct, if the realities of slavery, abolitionism, Reconstruction, disfranchisement, and segregation were as they described them, the Negroes *were* incapable of responsible citizenship, at least for the time being. The racism of the historians, however, came not from the realities of the episodes they described but from the assumptions they made about America. This nation, they assumed, is a white man's country. The white man's welfare is thus paramount to the Negro's, and race relations are properly controlled by whites. The ability to govern oneself, like other abilities which make up the capacity for civilization, can only be gradually acquired. Until Negroes acquire it they must accommodate themselves to the white man's wishes. To this end, laws and government can be used to coerce Negroes (but not whites) to accept changes in racial policy. The white man's superiority is evident in the civilization he has

---

[6]Claude Bowers, *The Tragic Era* (Cambridge, 1929), p. 307.

created. Negroes can benefit from contact with that civilization, but only under the firm tutelage of the white man.

In the second stage of its evolution, between the 1920's and 1954, segregationist thought changed significantly. During those years, anti-Negro ideas lost much of their scholarly authority and intellectual respectability and became the concern chiefly of emotional segregationists, most of whom were white Southerners. The change was gradual and is difficult to explain. Improved methodology and greater skepticism led scientists and social scientists to drop or mute their own racist views and challenge those of others, but this alone does not account for the change. Other factors contributed, but in amounts which are difficult to access. The environmentalism implicit in Progressive reform and the libertarian rhetoric accompanying the crusade to make the world safe for democracy disputed, though not always explicitly, the premises of anti-Negro racism. The Harlem Renaissance and the rise of a substantial Negro middle class made allegations of Negro inferiority less plausible. The emergence of such groups as the NAACP, the Urban League, and the Southern Conference on Human Welfare as viable organizations strengthened interracial cooperation and helped to make white Americans aware of the plight of Negroes. The postwar wave of racial violence evidenced greater militancy among Negroes, thereby undermining another racist stereotype and exposing the limitations of Ku Kluxery and demagoguery as bases for racial policy. Large-scale migration of Negroes to northern cities brought increased political power to the race as both Democrats and Republicans began competing for Negro votes; presently the federal government became more sympathetic to the race. The growing urbanization of both races created an environment in which anti-Negro ideas seemed more and more irrelevant to actual conditions. Passage of immigration restriction legislation in the early 1920's quieted the nativist movement in the East and the anti-Japanese movement on the West coast and deprived southern segregationists of an important ally with related interests.

In the 1930's and 1940's, European developments also influenced racial thought in America. For once, racists were embarrassed by excesses of their own kind as the implementation of Nazi racial theories made chillingly clear the consequences of rampant racism. Hitler's effort at genocide was repulsive to Americans, and one element of their reaction to it was the democratic, equalitarian ferment accompanying the effort to defeat the Axis powers.

The ferment did not subside with peace. It reached into scholarship, politics, and religion, and helped launch and sustain the Negro rights movement of the 1950's and 1960's. Segregationist thought was profoundly affected by it. Since 1954 there is a new racism in the land, built upon the foundations of the old, but different from it in significant respects. Perhaps its most curious feature is the revival of interest in scientific racism, a response by segregationists to the Supreme Court's use of social science authorities in the school integration decision, *Brown* v. *Board of Education of Topeka.* The new scientific racists have found it necessary to recast old ideas to meet a new national mood. The blatant racism of the past is not as efficacious as it once was. Today's racism is more subtle and indirect. Only extremists, who embarrass other segregationists, still insist that Negroes are absolutely inferior to whites, or openly justify violence and intimidation to keep the race subordinate. The emphasis now is on racial differences. Races are said to differ in relative abilities in different areas of endeavor. Thus whites might be superior in some areas—intelligence, reasoning, and adaptability to Western civilization, for example—and Negroes in others—rhythm, perspiration, and domestic art.

Historians have by and large dropped their racism, as recent works on slavery, abolitionists, and Reconstruction indicate, but eradicating the effects of their earlier views is a long, difficult process and not yet complete. Negro history is still ignored or imperfectly understood by most Americans, and occasionally segregationist stereotypes still appear in works by academic historians. In his textbook, *The South Since 1865,* published in 1963 by Macmillan, Professor John Samuel Ezell of the University of Oklahoma had this to say: "Negroes were widely used in tobacco factories. Most of the work called for little skill, while some of it needed rhythm, which the Negroes had [and the] all-pervading smell did not bother them."[7]

Southern segregationists have also altered their racism. Churchmen seem less sure than they once were that rigid segregation is "God's way" in race relations. Most large religious denominations in and out of the South have, at least abstractly, endorsed racial integration and interracial cooperation, but churches remain among the most segregated of American institutions. Politicians in the South no longer shout "Nigger, nigger"; while those in the North are sometimes out-

---

[7]John Samuel Ezell, *The South Since 1865* (New York, 1963), p. 145.

spoken in their dedication to Negro rights and racial equality, at least in the abstract. Too often, however, politicians and civic leaders in both sections conceal covert racism in talk of states' rights and local self-government. Other Americans both in and out of politics often accomplish the same end with talk of neighborhood schools and the sanctity of private property. The recent successes of the Negro rights movement and the emergence of militancy and black nationalism among some Negroes have provided a new occasion for segregationists to vent their anti-Negro views, but they usually do so in the language of indirection. The northern "backlash" to the Negro rights movement is more sophisticated and subtle than the old southern segregationists were. The distinction between racist and nonracist is therefore less obvious than it once was.

One other significant division in segregationist thought has persisted since 1890. That thought is not monolithic. It has existed on several levels of intensity, and its diversity has been increased by the fact that its proponents often have special axes to grind. Most of its proponents have been southern whites pragmatically interested in preserving segregation, disfranchisement, and white supremacy; a few have been race theorists expounding a general philosophy of interracial or interethnic relations. Some are extreme in their views, thoroughly contemptuous of Negroes and apologists for racial policies of the most repressive sort. Others are paternalists, men who regard themselves as friends of the race and applaud Negro advancement so long as the basic framework of segregation remains. Some are chiefly concerned with social segregation; their chief bugbear is an alleged threat of widespread racial intermarriage, which they warn is an imminent national catastrophy. Others talk chiefly of political equality, which they view as a likely back door to complete racial equality—and national degeneration. Despite significant areas of disagreement between extremists and paternalists and differences in emphasis between Northerners and Southerners, these groups all agreed that Negroes are inferior to whites and that segregation and white supremacy are desirable racial policies. As far as Negroes are concerned, then, the agreement between these groups is far more important than the disagreement.

The segregationist mentality is a composite of the features of segregationist thought. Those features, it is hoped, are illustrated in the items included in this collection, but it seems proper to summarize and comment briefly upon the more important of them.

Segregationist ideas do not exist in an intellectual vacuum. They are part of a larger cosmology. They assume a static, hereditarian view of human nature and social processes which leaves little room for environmentalism and social manipulation. Yet segregationists are not always orthodox conservatives, nor even reactionaries in the usual meaning of that term. Their professed conservatism is often compromised by a populistic radicalism which leads them to take the law into their own hands or to justify the actions of others who do. They flout the 14th and 15th Amendments while posturing as champions of the Constitution; they use government to oppress a minority while mouthing the libertarian rhetoric of the founding fathers. Their conservatism is thus eclectic, too eclectic to withstand logical analysis. The same is true of their hereditarianism. Only those qualities of human nature which perpetuate white supremacy are said to be hereditary in origin; all others are regarded as environmental. They exalt the white man's dislike for Negroes into a biological "consciousness of kind," while they view the Negro's desire for equality as evidence of his susceptibility to demagoguery.

This pattern of paradox and inconsistency is the cardinal feature of segregationist thought. It results in part from the facility with which segregationists compartmentalize their thinking and simultaneously hold contradictory convictions without conscious hypocrisy. Segregationists, or at least those who authored standard expositions of their ideas in this century, are not notable for their intellectuality. Few of them ever rationally examined their racial views. They regard themselves as practical men of affairs, as realists rather than ideologues or theoreticians, labels they reserve for equalitarians. At the same time, they boast of their allegiance to principles, especially what they call high moral principles. This failure to reconcile pragmatism and principle is one example of their tendency to speak in terms of principle when they have only specific incidents in mind. They often tailor their thinking to immediate needs without regard to larger philosophical considerations. For example, in *Briggs* v. *Elliott,* one of the cases covered by the school integration decision of 1954, segregationists argued that the effects of compulsory school integration would be worst at the elementary school level, involving as it would children "of very tender years." At the same time, in another of the cases, *Davis* v. *County School Board of Prince Edward County,* one of the witnesses called by the state of Virginia testified that he had "seen Negro children and white children go to school . . . at the elementary stages with very little difficulty." The witness Dr. Lindley Stiles, dean of the University of Virginia School of Education, also foresaw "very little problem" integrating colleges and graduate schools. It was only at the high school level that he expected difficulty. The difference in the testimony in the two cases reflects the fact that the former involved a challenge to elementary school segregation and the latter concerned segregation at the secondary level.[8]

As this indicates segregationists sometimes say different things to different audiences. In recent years, for example, the Mississippi Citizens' Councils have taken the lead in spreading ideas of scientific racism and assuring segregationists that the race policies of Mississippi rest upon clearly demonstrated scientific data. There is no equivocation on this subject in *The Citizen,* official publication of the Councils. Yet in discussing racial inequality in an address at Carleton College in Minnesota in 1962, William J. Simmons, editor of *The Citizen,* declared that "the question of race differences and their significance is far from having been settled in the research laboratory."[9] Apparently Simmons believed a moderate pose enhanced his credibility before a skeptical audience.

One explanation for this kind of opportunism is the fact that segregationists never had a recognized intellectual leader or theoretician with sufficient authority to impose order upon a mélange of conflicting views. No segregationist ever achieved the influence Madison Grant or Lothrop Stoddard once enjoyed among nativists. No work on white supremacy ever approached the authority and influence of Grant's *The Passing of the Great Race* (1921) or Stoddard's *The Rising Tide of Color* (1920). Earnest Sevier Cox' *White America* (1923), too much concerned with African colonization, was unread, while more recent efforts by Carleton Putnam, *Race and Reason* (1961) and *Race and Reality* (1967), lack the substance even of Grant or Stoddard's works. As a result, the segregationist ideology was never systematized, its paradoxes never resolved, its ultimate goals never reasoned through. (Much of what is now used to defend segregation was once used to justify slavery.) It was a jerry-built defense of southern race policies as those policies developed between 1890 and World War I. A makeshift of whim and whimsey, truth, half-truth, and untruth, opportunism and necessity, it alternately rationalizes violence, intimidation,

---

[8]See I. A. Newby, *Challenge to the Court* (Baton Rouge, 1967), pp. 49-50.

[9]W. J. Simmons, "The Race Problem Moves North," distributed by the Citizens' Councils, Jackson, Miss. (1962).

and paternalism. Segregationists alternately insist that Negroes prefer segregation and that it is necessary to take stern measures to keep them segregated. Segregationist thought is a body of ideas accepted on faith by those already emotionally committed to white supremacy. It appeals to true believers; it reassures the faithful, but has little appeal to the skeptic.

One of its notable features is the double standard. Negroes are judged by their race and individually faulted for the shortcomings of all Negroes, past and present. Whites, on the other hand, are judged as individuals. "It is idle to argue that all members of homo sapiens should be treated as individuals regardless of race," psychologist Henry E. Garrett, a leading apologist for white supremacy, wrote in 1961.[10] Thus Garrett can view political turmoil in Africa as evidence of the Negro's inability to govern himself, but can see no racial implications in the proclivity of whites in this century to wage periodic wars on a global scale.

A revealing instance of the double standard is the idea that Negroes must "earn" rights which whites receive automatically. Segregationists would circumscribe Negro voting and office holding until the race demonstrates (to their satisfaction) the capacity for self-government, and shunt Negro children into Jim Crow schools until they are satisfied that the IQ scores of Negroes match those of whites. Rarely, however, do they suggest ways in which equality might be earned. Indeed, if inequality results from genetic factors, as they allege, it can be overcome by evolution, which is to say it cannot be overcome at all, for as Negroes evolve (upward presumably), so also will whites. The Negro, alas, will never catch up! In this connection the segregationists' view of the current Negro rights movement is interesting. Through that movement, it would seem, Negroes are "earning" equality by overcoming all the obstacles whites are able to devise to keep them subjugated. To segregationists, however, the movement is merely a concerted effort by self-serving demagogues and liberal politicians to *give* favors to Negroes in exchange for votes on election day.

When carried to its logical conclusion, as it often is, the double standard leads to a denial of the obvious, and gives much of segregationist thought a quality of unreality. Consider the unreality of these typical statements: "in the essential struggle for existence the spirit of the South [toward Negroes] has been the spirit of kindliness and

---

[10]Henry E. Garrett, "The Scientific Racism of Juan Comas," *Mankind Quarterly,* Vol. II (October-December, 1961), p. 106.

helpfulness"; and "[the Southern Negro] by and large, does not want an end to segregation in itself any more than does the Southern white man."[11] Or consider the following statement made in 1965 by Gerrit Daams, a philosophy professor at Kent State University:

> Our society tends, on the average to demand more ability and performance from the whites than the Negroes for the same economic rewards. This is equivalent to the Negro having had, since a few decades prior to World War II, on the average, a better chance of attaining some desired socio-economic status level than does a white person of equal ability and performance. . . . On the average, the Negro is NOT required to be more able than a white person in order to get the same rewards. . . . White people in general are sympathetic to the underdog. Then, the skin color of the Negro aids in making him visible so as to draw the solicitous attention of white people, whereas the disadvantaged white man is more easily hidden and forgotten.[12]

These statements should not be dismissed as mere nonsense or hypocrisy. They indicate something deeper. Here is self-delusion so profound that language itself becomes its tool. Words take on their opposite meaning just as they did in George Orwell's *1984*. Carleton Putnam, perhaps the most influential disseminator of segregationist ideas today, recently summarized his defense of racial segregation in a pamphlet entitled "Framework for Love."

Politics has been the principal instrument for imposing and perpetuating segregation, and in politics segregationist thought has been most candidly expressed. Throughout the 20th century, segregationists have enjoyed the advantage of posturing as political and constitutional conservatives. In a nation wary of fundamental social change, they have had considerable success in branding their opponents "radicals," "visionaries," even "unAmerican." Fond of quoting the founding fathers and the Constitution, they appeal to what they term "the principles upon which America was founded and grew to greatness." The appeal is not without effect. Whatever the phrase "traditional American principles" might encompass, one of the most traditional of all American practices and one with which the founding fathers did not quarrel is white supremacy. Segregationists use this fact to insist that it is disinterested statesmanship on their part to use politics to

---

[11]The first statement is from Edgar Gardner Murphy, *Problems of the Present South* (New York, 1904), p. 184; the second is by Hodding Carter and is quoted in I. A. Newby, *op. cit.*, p. 39.

[12]Gerrit Daams, "Northern Professor Summarizes Reasons for Racial Segregation," *The Citizen*, Vol. IX (May, 1965, pp. 12-20. *The Citizen* is the official journal of the Citicens' Councils of America.

defend the status quo (that is, to buttress segregation), but crass selfishness and petty politics to use the political arena to promote integration or Negro advancement.

Segregationists have a restrictive view of government, or rather profess to have. It is more accurate to say they have a restrictive view of those governmental powers which threaten their racial policies. Their concern with limiting government is in fact an effort to limit the power of government to promote integration or racial equality. They insist that government has no legitimate power to help Negroes, but has every power to keep the race segregated and subordinate. Segregationists can use government to advance their racial interests, but integrationists can not. Where, they ask in all their literalism, does the Constitution specify that Negroes are entitled to integration? To which one can only reply, where does it specify that whites are entitled to segregation?

Segregationists rationalize these ideas by assuming, first, that government should coerce the individual as little as possible, and second, that segregation is the natural relationship between races and therefore not coercive. Thus, according to their logic, segregation maximizes freedom. Enforced integration is a form of "legal compulsion which cannot be tolerated in a free society," Professor Garrett has written,[13] oblivious to the irony in his statement. Democracy rests upon restraint. "Might and court decrees," psychologist Charles C. Josey of Butler University wrote recently in criticism of the *Brown* decision, "cannot engender love, friendship, goodwill, and righteousness, or even justice when they ignore the rights, wishes, and ideals of larger segments of the population."[14] He, too, missed the irony.

Proponents of these ideas rarely criticize democratic ideals, but implicit in their ideology is a denial of the substance of democracy. They defend segregation, disfranchisement, and discrimination—in the language of liberal democracy. They advocate what amounts to systematic repression of a minority—in the pose of libertarians and New Testament Christians. They speak endlessly of freedom, individualism, liberty, and self-government, but make them synonymous with segregation. The democracy they endorse is elitist, after the model of ancient Athens. This is what the republicanism of the

---

[13]Henry E. Garrett and Wesley C. George, letter to editor, *Science*, February 28, 1964, p. 913.

[14]Charles C. Josey, *An Inquiry Concerning Racial Prejudice* (New York, 1965), p. 28.

founding fathers means to them. They regard themselves as embattled defenders of democracy and the American way of life, and their motive, in their own view, is unselfish. "White supremacy," said a Georgia Congressman in 1923, "is not oppressive tyrannical supremacy, but is compassionate, God-like supremacy, exercised for the good of our nation, the happiness of the human race, and the civilization of the world."[15]

It is paradoxical that a set of ideas as weak and contradictory as those described above should appeal so enduringly to white Americans. Several explanations for this paradox suggest themselves. Segregation and attendant discriminations against Negroes were economically advantageous to many whites, and more or less satisfactory as a means of race control. They appealed to the vanity of whites and rationalized their status anxieties and feelings of inferiority. These are important factors which are commonly discussed by historians and others attempting to explain the persistence of anti-Negro racism in America. Since they are often discussed and their significance is apparent, we might profitably focus upon other factors which usually receive less attention. One of these is the traditional weakness of equalitarianism. Before the 1950's, pro-Negro sentiment in America was not always well articulated; equalitarian groups were small and poorly financed, and had difficulty reaching a national audience. Whites not openly hostile to Negroes were indifferent to their plight, and unaware that the nation even had a race problem. They associated race problems with significant outbursts of racial violence. Where there was no violence, they assumed, there was no problem. Few whites were thoroughgoing equalitarians, especially when it came to crucial issues of social equality and intermarriage.

The principal reason for the persistence of anti-Negro racism and concomitant policies of segregation and discrimination is historical—they are too elemental and vigorous a part of the national heritage to die of their own accord. American society has always been structured along white supremacy lines, and Americans absorb the racial values of their society just as they do its economic, political, and social values. Public policy has almost always given legal, institutional support to the idea that race is a proper basis for social classification. Our society has told whites that theirs is a superior race whose domination of racial policy is justified. It has told Negroes that theirs is a

[15]U.S. *Cong. Record,* 67th Cong., 4th sess., March 3, 1923, 5414. The speaker quoted was Rep. William C. Lankford.

race apart, inferior and contemptible, whose very presence is a national problem.

Here are the practical consequences of anti-Negro racism and a major reason for its endurance. Segregation creates a vicious cycle, a self-fulfilling prophecy. Its consequences become its justification. White Americans think of their national experience as a success story. America to them is a land of hope and opportunity, of economic abundance, social mobility, political equality. They see their society as one which cultivates initiative, individualism, self-reliance, self-sacrifice. They see America as a nation whose institutions are benevolent: the law protects everyone from oppression and is not itself oppressive; the fundamental rights of citizens are spelled out in the Constitution and guaranteed to all; the right of trial by an impartial jury of one's peers is so basic as to be a commonplace; every man respects his fellowman, his person and property, his womenfolk and children, his freedom of expression and movement. This picture of course is overdrawn in the popular imagination, but there is an element of truth in it for whites.

For Negroes the story is different. For them those ideals are honored more in the breach than the observance. Since 1890 Negroes have been relegated to a world of more or less rigid segregation and a deadening second-class status that saps the energies of all but the most persevering. The racial meaning of this must be understood. Segregation is the most important fact in the history of Negro Americans in this century, dominating their experience as political freedom, economic opportunity, and social mobility dominated the white man's. Segregation excluded Negroes from what whites call the American way of life. It tended to cultivate in them personal and social traits, moral and ethical values, which add up to a way of life notably different from that of whites. Not all Negroes were so affected, but there was a tendency in this direction. Measured by the standards of the larger society, the "good" white American was one who displayed initiative, daring, independence; the "good" Negro one who was imitative, humble, ingratiating, childlike, a sycophant or a clown. The Negro's experience did not reward thrift and self-sacrifice as the white man's did. It offered him little hope for a better tomorrow. It encouraged irresponsibility, ignorance, servility, helplessness, hopelessness, qualities which white Americans despised. His political and social status was ill designed to inculcate respect for law and government, for property rights, middle-class morality, the family, even his fellow Negroes. To him, government often seemed little more than organized tyranny, the law a device for denying him the fruits of his labor, society a system permitting his womenfolk to be compromised, his children exploited, his honor and self-respect undermined.

Again, the *racial* significance of this must be stressed. For whites, segregation was not even an inconvenience; for Negroes, it made race the supreme fact of life. At every turn it subjected the Negro to an invidious racial test. A ubiquitous racial veil circumscribed his liberties, stifled his talents, thwarted his ambition. He found it impossible, or virtually so, to exercise the responsibilities of citizenship or reap the rewards of the good life. He could not protect himself, his family, his property. He could not readily achieve a position of self-respect, independence, virtue.

What this means is that segregation creates ostensibly objective evidence to corroborate the segregationist view of Negroes. That at least is the conclusion white Americans have reached. Whites seem everywhere superior to Negroes. They are better educated, live better, control the instruments of power and prestige. Negroes seem too often to deviate from acceptable standards of conduct. They become, in the view of whites, a race prone to violence, illegitimacy, venereal disease, and broken homes, a people who threaten property values, make low scores on intelligence tests, and lower standards in public schools.

The impact of this has been overwhelming. White Americans are preconditioned to think of Negroes in racial terms, and they accordingly conclude that the Negro's condition is explainable only in those terms. Thus white attitudes toward Negroes have always reflected the status of the race in this country, varying from time to time and section to section according to the status or condition of Negroes in a given time or section. It is easy here to overstate cause and effect and oversimplify a complex phenomenon, but the history of anti-Negro thought in America seems to follow this pattern: after Negroes achieve or are relegated to a certain status, whites then develop a systematic rationale to justify that status. Only after Negroes were enslaved did white Americans conclude that slavery was the natural status of the race, and only after the slave system came under systematic abolitionist attack were the most elaborate scientific, historical, and scriptural authorities cultivated to legitimate it. When Negroes were segregated. the process occurred again. Racists then recognized segregation as the natural status for Negroes, and again cultivated authorities to support their conclusion.

The slow liberalization of racial ideas over the last generation has followed closely upon the rise of a Negro middle class, the emergence of independent black Africa, and new or heightened Negro achievement in many areas. The most excessive claims of Negro inferiority are no longer tenable, and have disappeared from all but the most extreme anti-Negro literature. The difficulty is that white attitudes are changing more slowly than Negro achievement and the aspiration that achievement inspires. If this analysis is correct, whites will not believe essentially in racial equality until the Negro actually achieves equality. Only then will the fallacies of anti-Negro thought be apparent. But the major obstacle to Negro equality is the white man's belief in inequality and the complex of racial policies which rest upon that belief. The way out of this impasse would seem to involve social changes fundamental enough to enable Negroes to achieve actual equality. This, however, would require whites to devise social policies which run counter to deeply held racial convictions. That they will do so, with or without further violence, is problematical. The traditions of racism are strong and enduring. As a white Southerner of moderate racial views once said, "the problem is not the negro, but the white man's attitude toward the negro."[16]

---

[16]Thomas Pearce Bailey, *Race Orthodoxy in the South* (New York, 1914), p. 37.

The Race Question
in the United States:
An Overview in 1890

JOHN T. MORGAN

In 1890 the South stood at the threshold of a revolution in race relations. Within two decades, segregationists had radically altered the legal and constitutional status of Negroes there, and the fortunes of the race had plummeted. The advent of segregation and disfranchisement meant the triumph of white supremacy and of the racial ideas it represented. In the following article, written in 1890, Senator John T. Morgan of Alabama summarizes the arguments just then crystallizing in defense of the new racial policies. His article is a convenient resume of segregationist ideas at the outset of the era of segregation and disfranchisement. It introduces, in one form or another, the typical arguments in favor of white supremacy, arguments which even today comprise a considerable part of the segregationist ideology. It also illustrates the twisted logic of segregationists and the basic assumptions they make about race relations in America: that races are innately unequal, that race prejudice is natural and instinctive, that race mixture is biologically unwise and socially degrading, that America is a white man's country in which white men will—and should—control race policy, that Negroes are incapable of effective citizenship, that the race has retrogressed since emancipation, that history, science and religion support white supremacy, that disfranchisement does no violence to American democracy, that the future welfare of America depends upon the preservation of segregation and white racial purity, and that for all these reasons extreme measures are justified in preserving white supremacy.

*Reprinted from John T. Morgan, "The Race Question in the United States," *Arena,* Vol. II (September, 1890), pp. 385-98.

The social and political questions connected with the African race, in the United States, all relate to and depend upon the essential differences between the negro and the white man, as they have been arranged by the hands of the Creator.

Amongst these differences, the color of the skin, while it distinguishes the races unmistakably, is the least important. The mental differences and differing traits, including the faculty of governing, forecast, enterprise, and the wide field of achieving in the arts and sciences, are accurately measured by the contrast of the civilization of the United States, with the barbarism of Central Africa.

[The race problem today is not a consequence of Negro slavery.] If the negroes in the United States were not descended from a people who enslaved them and sold them into foreign bondage, and who are still engaged in the same traffic; if they had been invited to this country to become citizens and to contribute what talents and virtues they have to the conduct of our complex system of government,— the race question would still be as much a vital and unavoidable issue, political and social, as it is under the existing and widely different conditions.

It is the presence of seven or eight millions of negroes in this country and the friction caused by their political power and their social aspirations, and not the fact that they were recently in slavery, that agitates and distresses the people of both races. If they were not in the United States, there would be perfect peace and harmony amongst the people.

There is a decided aversion between the white race and the Indian, —a race who has never submitted to enslavement. The difference in color and in social traits sufficiently accounts for this aversion, which exists in spite of our admiration for them as a brave and independent race. Has it been long persistence in a course of injustice and ill usage that has caused this aversion, or is it the race aversion that has caused the ill usage and retaliations that have filled the fairest valleys of our country with massacre and havoc? . . . In the history of the Indians we find the most conclusive proofs that no race, inferior in capacity and intelligence, can co-exist with the white race, in the same government, and preserve its distinctive traits, or social organization. If the two races cannot merge, and sink their individuality, by a commingling of blood, the inferior race will be crushed. . . .

The negro race in their native land, have never made a voluntary and concerted effort to rise above the plane of slavery; they have not contributed a thought, or a labor, except by compulsion, to aid the progress of civilization. Nothing has emanated from the negroes of Africa, in art, science, or enterprise that has been of the least service to mankind. Their own history at home, demonstrates their inferiority when compared with that of other peoples.

They have been, for ages, the possessors of a fertile country, where they have bred in myriads, and no foreign power has attempted to subjugate them.[1] The result of their contributions to the wealth of the world is limited to slaves, and the natural productions of the forests. They have no agricultural implement, except a rude, iron hoe; no ships for the seas and no beasts of burden. Their social development has never risen so high as to repress human sacrifices and cannibalism; while their religion is a witchcraft that is attended with every brutal crime.

The inferiority of the negro race, as compared with the white race, is so essentially true, and so obvious, that to assume it in argument, cannot be justly attributed to prejudice. If it is prejudice, it is rare prejudice, which affects nearly all the white race, and proves the existence of a deep-seated race aversion. . . Whether the law that created this aversion is natural, or contrary to nature; whether it is of human or divine origin; whether it is wicked, or good,—it equally affects and controls both races in all their relations, and it is immutable,—grounded in convictions and sentiments that neither race can yield. . . .

Marriages have seldom occurred between Chinese or Malays, or Indians, and the negro race; and by the universal decree of the white race, such marriages are prohibited. No expression of race aversion could be more distinct than this.

This race aversion has been greatly increased in this country by the abolition of slavery. The trust and confidence felt by the slaves toward their former masters has [sic] been largely supplanted by a feeling of resentment, which politicians are rapidly converting into hatred and revenge. This condition would not have been so pronounced, if the negro race had not been forced, unprepared and disqualified [sic], into the exercise of full rights and powers incident to citizenship. That unwise and unnecessary decree has caused the aversion between the races to infuse its virus into the social and political

---

[1]In 1890 all of Africa except Liberia and Ethiopia was claimed and controlled in greater or lesser degree by the major European powers. The entire continent, its human as well as its natural resources, was thus exploited for Europe's and the white man's advantage.

affairs of the country, where it will be, forever, a rankling poison. It has intensified into a race conflict all political questions, in localities where there are large negro populations. It is discussed and voted upon everywhere, from the national capital to the ballot box; exciting the most acrimonious debates and extreme measures of legislation. . . .

The race conflict in the United States is, essentially a social controversy, aggravated by its union with the government of the country.

Race conflicts have attended the entire history of English-speaking people. Having, as they believe, a mission and leadership in the civilization of barbarous people and in all the progress of mankind, they have not permitted the inferior races to check their movements.

Our North American history is filled with illustrations of this unrelenting progress.[2] By the destruction of the implacable Indian, we have possessed ourselves of his inheritance,—the fairest and richest in the world. He would not be a slave, and we drove him out and filled his place with negroes found in bondage in their native land, and imported as slaves. The patient, thrifty Chinaman was found to be depraved. He was invited to come here under full protection. When he became the successful rival of our laboring classes and encumbered our industries with a competition that starved the people who refused to admit him to their family circle as an equal, we summarily decreed his banishment.[3] . . .

The slave laws held the negro to his daily work; made him temperate; enforced subordination; repressed crime and misdemeanor; and made him a safe and harmless neighbor. There was no cause for political or social rivalry with the white people, who labored, or with any other class, and, while the slave did not aspire to such an attitude, the white man did not condescend to it. While the slaves were under the strict dominion of their masters, no class of people were better secured against interference, by other people, with their rights, of any kind. The result was that there was neither rivalry nor friction between the laboring classes in the South.

There was instinctive race aversion between them, which nothing could prevent, or modify, except the inferior position of the negro,

---

[2]Here is illustrated the segregationists' tendency to view history strictly from the white man's vantage point. "Progress" is equated with "destruction" of Indians, enslavement of Negroes, and exclusion of "the Chinaman" from America.

[3]The Chinese Exclusion Act of 1882 barred Chinese immigration to the United States. It was the first immigration exclusion act in the nation's history.

which neutralized all personal jealousies. This inferiority and dependence excited, in all classes of white people, that sort of Christian benevolence that compassionates, always, the poorest and least attractive of the human family. The Christian training of the negro race in the South is the undesirable [sic] proof of this state of sentiment towards them.

When this race aversion was excited by the apprehensions of the nonslaveholders, of the possibility of the future social equality, or union of the races, under political pressure, it flamed up into angry abhorrence, and has become a settled antagonism, as these apprehensions have been realized. It was this apprehension, and not any coercion or other fear of consequences that, above all other considerations, incited, armed, fed with the bread earned by the toil of women in the fields, clothed with their skill, and sent to the Southern armies, the sturdiest and most resolute of that wonderful body of citizen soldiery. Knowing all that this political movement meant and fully comprehending its results, these men felt that any sacrifice they could make, to prevent race equality in the South, could not outweigh their duty to their families, their race, and their country. . . .

It was the hope and expectation of the abolitionists who, as humanitarians, were also enthusiasts, that the emancipation of the negro would cure the alleged conflict between free and slave labor; that freedom would qualify the negro race for unobstructed social intercourse with the white race; and that the ballot would force them into such political influence as to compel the abolition, also, of race aversion and social discrimination. The ballot in the hands of the negro has had just the contrary effect. It has been relied upon as a substitute for personal worth, industry, and good conduct, to lift the inferior race to the same plane with the superior race; but it has constantly exposed the negro race to organized political opposition, and has chilled the hopes and balked the efforts of those who most desired to help the negroes to profit by their freedom.

The negroes have uniformly used the ballot as a means of inflicting the penalties of resentment and race animosity upon southern people. They seem incapable of conceiving that their political power has any other valuable use than as an expression of hatred and ill will towards their former owners. The history of Hayti and Jamaica, on the other hand, has not been forgotten in the southern states. The people there understand that prudence has restrained the excesses that destroyed, or drove out, the white race, from these and other islands of the

West Indies, for the same reasons that now animate the negroes and unite them, in solid political movement, in hostility to the white race. This strenuous and constant antagonism of the negro race towards the white people of the South, has compelled them, also, to unite on race lines for security.[4]

[During Radical Reconstruction] the first movement of the negro party in the South, and of their white leaders there and in Congress, was directed to the vital point of securing race equality, in social as well as political privileges, by the compulsion of law. The negro race, flattered by this effort, with the hope, that is most keenly indulged by every negro of mixed blood, of being foisted into the white families, freely contributed its entire political power to assist in such robbery of States and people, as never was practiced under the authority of law. The warnings of this experience cannot be ignored or forgotten. It is impossible to divide the negro race on any political question, and whatever measure they will support or oppose will first be tested by the race issue.[5] . . .

What is the cause of this condition of the negro race in the United States, which their power and political influence has not been able to remove, but has only aggravated? The answer is recorded in the home history of every white family in the United States. The negro race cannot be made homogeneous with the white race. It is the abhorrence that every white woman in our country feels towards the marriage of her son or daughter with a negro, that gives the final and conclusive answer to this question. Wealth, character, abilities, accomplishments and position, have no effect to modify this aversion of the white woman to a negro-marital alliance. Men may yield to such considerations, or to others of a baser sort; but the snows will fall from heaven in sooty blackness, sooner than the white woman of the United States will consent to the maternity of negro families. It will become more and more the pride of the men of our race to resist any movement, social or political, that will promote the unwelcome intrusion of the negro race into the white family circle.

---

[4]Here as elsewhere segregationists blame Negroes for racial antipathy in the South.

[5]Here is an interesting application of the segregationists' double standard. The problem with Negro voting, says Morgan, is that Negroes judge political issues according to their racial (i.e., group) self-interest. This of course would seem to indicate that Negroes *do* understand political issues, and do what other interest groups in American politics have always done— judge political issues in terms of group or individual interest. Certainly this is what segregationists and white supremacists were doing, even as Morgan wrote. The senator had no objection to whites judging political issues by racial considerations. But for Negroes to do likewise was in his view a threat to the general welfare and justification for disfranchisement.

This is the central and vital point in the race question. If the negroes, being our equals in political privileges, could be absorbed into our race, as equals, there would be no obstacle to our harmonious and beneficent association, in this free country, but neither laws, nor any form of constraint, can force the doors to our homes and seat them at our firesides.

The voting power is the only reliance of the negro for lifting his race to the level of the social union or equality with the white race. The race jealousy that the exertion of that power inflames, has united the white race on the color line, in every State where there is a dense negro population, and has moved other communities, that have no fear of negro domination, to feel for those who are threatened with this calamity, the warmest of sympathy. . . .

Ours is a representative government, with the sovereignty residing in the people; and those who exert the powers of sovereignty are chosen for that purpose, not by the people at large, but by qualified voters. One in about every five of our population is qualified by the law to represent himself and the four other persons in the group, in voting at elections. This arbitrary arrangement imposes no restraint upon the voter, as to how he will represent his group, except his sense of justice, his friendship for the race he represents, or his natural affections and love of country. He has no other than a remote, moral responsibility to his non-voting constituency; and he measures his duty to them by his more direct allegiance to his party. Four fifths of the people of the United States are thus arbitrarily represented in the ballot box, by the one-fifth who are qualified voters.[6]

This seemingly dangerous power of the voter is based upon the theory of the representation in the ballot box of that sacred relation which inspires the honest and intelligent voter with the most dutiful and quickened sense of trust and natural affection—the family relation. Controlled by such influences, this power becomes the most conservative and the best element in a government for the people. But the danger of injecting into the voting power a feeling of race aversion, or hostility, is obvious. It could scarcely be over-stated. It cannot be too carefully avoided in the government of the country. The family is the real unit of our power in free government.

While the families of our country are homogeneous, there is little

---

[6]The reader will no doubt note the striking resemblance between Morgan's justification for Negro disfranchisement and the theory of "virtual representation" advanced by some English Tories against American colonists who were crying "no taxation without representation" in the years prior to the American Revolution.

danger that the voters who represent them will war upon their security, or fail to be loyal to their best interests. But where the voters, who represent one fifth of the political power of the entire country (and, in some of the States, have a majority), are excluded by reason of race, or caste, or their previous slavery, from family relationships with the minority [sic], it is certain that resentment, prejudices, and hostility will animate them; and they will vote to humiliate and destroy that part of their constituency. . . . It seems to be clear, that there is extreme danger, under existing conditions, in confiding to negro voters the representation of white families in the ballot box.

This is the real race question, in politics, that has vexed our people from the beginning. . . .

The practical phase of the question is, whether the white race can be made to include the negro race in a free and honest welcome into their families, as "men and brethren." There are some enthusiasts, claiming to be exalted humanitarians, who advocate the solution of this difficulty by raising the negro race to the social level of the white race through legislative expedients that look to the mingling of the blood of the races; but this is far from being the sentiment of the great body of the people of the United States. They understand the impossibility of such a result. The full-blooded negroes also understand it, and hesitate, if they do not refuse, to make this effort. "The Afro-Americans," as the mulattoes describe themselves, believe that a precedent has been set, by their foremost men, which they can follow, with the aid of the politicians, that will secure their incorporation, by marriage, into the white families of the country. These vain expectations will be followed with the chagrin of utter disappointment, and will increase their discontent.

Every day the distance increases between these races, and they are becoming more jealous and intolerant of each other. This condition is disclosed in the schools, churches, and in every industrial pursuit. The field for negro labor, except in the heaviest drudgery and in menial occupations, is constantly narrowing, until their presence is not tolerated in the higher commercial pursuits, or in the use of important corporate franchises. This is more distinctly the result of race aversion than is the exclusion of the Chinese from our country. The political power given to the negro race, no matter how they may use it, only increases race antagonism. That power, has so far, greatly aggravated the opposition to them. It can never make their presence in this country, which has always been a cause of dissension, welcome to the white people.

Science and the
"Negro Problem"

JAMES BARDIN

A major tenet of segregationist thought is that racial policy must rest upon scientific truth. The trouble with racial reformers and equalitarians, or so segregationists often complain, is their propensity to view racial issues in ethical and humanitarian terms. They thereby lose sight of racial—and scientific—realities, and the reforms they propose are therefore unworkable. The following article, by Professor James Bardin, M.D., of the University of Virginia, exemplifies this important feature of the segregationist ideology. Like many other segregationists who were also scientists, he discussed what is really an emotional and moral issue in an ostensibly detached manner, and thereby convinced himself that he had no racial "prejudice." Today we think of segregationists as unreasoning, emotional bigots. It is important to remember, however, that in their own minds, segregationists are rational, even detached, in their approach to race problems. They are convinced that their primary loyalty is to truth, and that they have the interests of all races and sections of the country at heart. In their view it is not segregationists, but racial reformers, who are the central element in the racial problem.

. . . . In the thought of the average southerner, the uplift of the Negro has a radically different significance, usually, from that which it has in the thought of those living outside the south, who do not altogether understand southern social conditions.

First and foremost, the southern man is interested in raising the economic value of the Negro. To accomplish this various means have been adopted, all designed to train the Negro in things of practical

---

*Reprinted from James Bardin, "The Psychological Factor in Southern Race Problems," New York: Science Press, 1913.

usefulness. Concomitantly, the churches and philanthropical institutions are working toward the same end by attempting to teach the Negroes how to live better, and thus increase their efficiency and insure their status as self-supporting, independent members of society. The Negroes themselves are working to accomplish this end in practically every institution maintained by them throughout the south. This view of the Negro problem, practical in the extreme, is the one generally held at present in the south. The ideal seems to be to force the Negro to earn a better place in society and political life by the sweat of his brow and the toil of his hands; which toil, it is confidently hoped, will be guided by a constantly increasing intelligence, itself the indirect fruit of his labor.

On the other hand, outside the south the Negro problem is generally viewed as not primarily an economic, but as a political and "social rights" problem. The aim of many, if not most, of those living outside the south who take an active interest in the Negro is to secure for him fuller political rights and wider social opportunities, believing that as restrictions are removed, the Negro's position will improve in every respect, and he will ultimately take his place side by side with the whites, on an equal footing and possessing an identical cultural equipment.

Whatever be the theoretical merit of these views, whatever be the results of their trial, whatever be the advantage of one over the other ethically, it can easily be seen that although they advocate almost exactly opposite methods, those who advocate them are striving to reach the same goal. Each group is attempting to help the Negro to attain a more complete civilization; and each is attempting to do this by trying to make the Negro absorb the white man's civilization and come into complete accord with the profound moving-springs of the white man's social sanctions.

Many writers have contributed to the elaboration of these prevailing views of the problem. Admittedly, all of them have as their ideal the creation through evolutionary processes of a state in which the whites and the Negroes live side by side, each group partaking of the same civilization on a basis of ethical equality, and each playing its part in government and society according to its ability. This bi-racial state, theoretically, should have a single civilization, common to and understood similarly by both peoples; this civilization—and here is the vital point—will be the civilization of the whites, which, it is assumed, will be inculcated into the Negroes and which the Negroes will absorb without sufficiently modifying it to impair its usefulness as a foundation for a complex, though organically homogeneous, society.

Underlying the conception of a state such as has just been described lies a more fundamental conception which is seldom formulated, but upon which the whole structure of theory about southern race problems is based. This conception may be stated in various ways; its boldest, most general, and most erroneous form is the hypothesis that "all men are equal"; a more moderate form is "equal opportunity for all, special privilege for none"; but the most comprehensive form, which contains by implication very nearly all that is included in our thought upon the matter, is that "all men, when normal, possess the same capacity for intelligence and the same ability to absorb culture and to become civilized"; in other words, that all men are essentially alike mentally and morally, when viewed in the large, notwithstanding physical and physiological differences. The culture of any group of men, it is assumed, may be adopted by, or forced upon any other group of men, without effecting any revolutionary change in the culture. It is tacitly thought that while the processes of evolution have given one race a white skin and another race a black skin, have made one race relatively resistant to tuberculosis and the other relatively susceptible, and so on, the minds of both are alike—have not diverged as their bodies have in the evolutionary series—and that the mental processes of one may become, by proper direction, the mental processes of the other.

On conventional ethical grounds, the hypothesis of human equality can not be assailed. The Christian world, particularly that part of it which really thinks, is essentially altruistic, and this altruism demands that all men be given the fullest and most equal opportunities to get the best out of life. But it is seldom realized that this is an ideal, not a working formula; that it is, further, an ethical ideal, not a scientific one.[1] Out of this misconception of the ideal of human equality have sprung many grievous and oftentimes dangerous fallacies, chief among which are two: (1) that all men possess the same potentialities for culture; and (2) that a so-called "higher culture" may and ethically

---

[1] Bardin's purpose was to achieve and maintain scientific objectivity. It should be noted, however, that he achieved objectivity merely by banishing ethics, morality, and altruism from his discussion of race and racial policy. Segregationists often do this; it removes some troublesome questions of ethics and morality from the formulation of racial policy and from personal dealings with Negroes. Here as elsewhere segregationists label whatever serves their needs "scientific" and "objective," and everything else "idealistic" and therefore impractical.

should be substituted for a so-called "lower culture" whenever opportunity presents itself.

As has been said, each of these ideas has a basis in ethical principles. But both are fallacious when scientifically considered. Each assumes too much, and each tries to make out of an ethical ideal the scientific working formula for the uplifting of backward people. Neither takes into account that culture and civilization are as much the products of evolution as a white skin or a black skin.

Culture, in its broadest sense, is a phenomenon of race.[2] Even in our more or less homogeneous western European and American culture, racial differences are to be observed; if this were not true, why should we take the trouble to call some people Germans and others Spaniards, some Danes and others Italians? Yet, despite these evident differences, western European and American culture is a definite, characteristic thing, and underlying it we recognize a common stock of traditions and general ideas which have come down through the ages "in the blood," so to speak. The white-skinned peoples of western Europe and America all have approximately the same origin, in that through the remote mixing of a few strains of blood the modern racial types were set; and since then the peoples of western Europe have given evidence of their biological kinship by displaying approximately similar reactions to similar environmental conditions and to the influence of general ideas and movements of thought. Whatever variations have appeared in the physical and psychical types among the various peoples are due to differences in the mixtures of the original strains of blood, with the accompanying differences in the contributions of hereditary mental predispositions received by the respective peoples, plus subsequent adaptations to environmental conditions. But behind all the differences lies a common kinship of blood and of tradition, which has operated to produce the unit we call western European culture; and this racial kinship is the principal

---

[2]This idea of the relationship between culture and civilization on the one hand and race on the other was first developed systematically by the French race theorist Arthur de Gobineau, in *The Inequality of Human Races,* trans. Adrian Collins (London, 1915); originally published as *Essai sur l'inégalité des races humaines* (Paris, 1853-55), 4 vols. The idea enjoyed considerable scientific respectability at the time Bardin wrote this essay (1913), though there was no valid scientific evidence to corroborate it (nor is there any now). It is an example of the segregationists' use of inference. For example: races differ widely in physical appearance, and the civilizations of Europe (Caucasians), Africa (Negroes), and Asia (Mongolians) also differ widely. It is logical, reasoned segregationists, to infer from this that races differ psychically and that these psychical differences explain differences in culture and civilization.

reason why it is not difficult for one group of western Europeans to adopt without revolutionizing it the culture of another group. Furthermore, as a powerful factor assisting in the formation and growth of this western European culture, and aiding constantly in keeping it homogeneous, is the fact that the several strains of blood, particularly in the higher levels of society where most of the productive thinking is done, are incessantly mixing, and there are being interchanged incessantly, through heredity, the mental predispositions peculiar to the groups thus crossing. The people of western Europe and the white portion of American population, for the most part, are a sort of "blend" of similar racial stocks, presenting similar though not identical biological characteristics; and the varieties of this "blend," expressed in such terms as "English," "Dutch," and so forth, are due to differences in the numerical relationships of the contributing stocks forming these peoples. So, too, western European culture is a sort of "blend" of cultures, and the varieties of this "blend" parallel the varieties in the physical characteristics of the various peoples.

. . . Exactly the same statements apply to the Negroes. They have, physically and mentally, definite and easily recognizable characteristics, indicative of a common origin different from our own, and expressed in a similarity of Negro cultures throughout the world.

The fact of race as a physical and mental phenomenon is evident to every one. The peoples of the world differ, and often differ fundamentally; and these differences are ineradicable as long as the strain of blood remains unimpaired. On the physical side, this principle has long been an axiom. "Can the Ethiopian change his skin?" asks Jeremiah. We can not, do what we will with environment, change to any appreciable extent our anatomical make-up. A Chinaman's skin will remain yellow, a Negro's skin will remain black, no matter what we may do to alter them, so long as the races remain pure. The only way we can modify the color of the skin or the facial angle or texture of the hair in any great number of individuals is by crossing with another race. And the product of this crossing, should it become permanent, is a different race.

From the point of view of psychology, on the other hand, we have assumed that this principle is not true. We know that we cannot change a Negro's physical characteristics, so as to make him like ourselves, by bringing him to live among us. But we believe we can change his mental characteristics. In other words, while we are certain that we can not change the Negro's facial angle, we are equally certain that we can change his mental angle and make it like our own; while we consider it absurd to think that we can do anything to make the Negro's physical skin become white, we believe firmly that we can make the psychical analogue of his skin exactly like our own.

But is this a fact? Racial psychology says no. Mental character-istics are as distinctly and as organically a part of a race as its physi-cal characteristics, and for the same reason: both depend ultimately upon anatomical structure. Racial mental-set, racial ways of thinking, racial reactions to the influence of ideas, are as characteristic and as recognizable as racial skin-color and racial skull-conformation. This does not mean that mental characteristics and superficial anatomical characteristics necessarily bear any relationship to each other, as has sometimes been assumed; that is to say, the shape of the head, the weight of the brain, the cranial capacity, the length of the arms, the arrangement of the muscles in the calf of the leg, do not determine mental characteristics; physical and mental characteristics are, how-ever, parallel expressions of the particular evolutionary process which has resulted in the formation of a race; each set of characters is the specific result, in different structures, of the evolutionary process. Ultimately, mental differences must depend upon anatomical and physiological differences; but these differences are differences in the structure of the brain itself. If we are to assume any relationship whatsoever between brain and mind (and such a relationship, what-ever it may be, certainly exists), we must assume some anatomical and physiological differences in brains if we are to account for mental differences.

The more the races of men are studied, the more certain becomes the evidence to show that races have characteristic mental peculiari-ties, which would serve to distinguish species and varieties almost as well as physical characteristics. In practical life, in jurisprudence, in language itself, we empirically allow for these racial mental differ-ences. But we have never taken the trouble to study them nor to understand their nature from a scientific point of view, and almost nothing is known about their potentialities.[3]

Taking as a fact these mental differences, let us for a moment consider the possibility of their modification. It has been pointed out that mental differences must ultimately depend upon material

---

[3]Here Bardin admits in effect that he has no scientific data to support his views about racial psychology.

anatomical differences in brain structure; if we deny this, we instantly remove racial psychology from the field of science to that of metaphysics, and controvert all the observed data of physiological psychology; there must be some structural differences between the brain of a Negro and that of a white man, though such differences are admittedly very hard to detect by present methods. We know that it is impossible for us to modify anatomical structures at will; we can undoubtedly change them (within narrow limits, by selection of characters already present and the accentuation of these), but we can not make any two differing anatomical characters become exactly alike. Why, then, should we assume that we can modify at will the mental processes of a race, since these mental processes are expressions of a certain definite anatomical and physiological organization, which we know can not be altered save by the crossing of bloods or by the laborious and infinitely slow processes of evolution?

Yet, north and south, we wish to do this very thing, and to do it in its extreme form. For we are not merely trying to change the direction of the Negro's peculiar mental characteristics, and to improve them by selection among the elements already present—we are trying, on the contrary, to deprive the Negro of his own racial mental characteristics, and to substitute our own in their place, *at the same time keeping him anatomically a Negro.* That this is an impossibility follows after the former argument.

It will undoubtedly be said, by way of refutation, that the Negroes of the southern states have advanced and advanced considerably since they have been in this country. This is unreservedly true. But it is often forgotten that they have advanced as Negroes, not as anything else. They have adopted the form of our civilization and to a certain extent (due principally to the influence of language), the mould of our thought. But however much the form of the civilization and the mould of the thought resemble our own, the substance of both is different. The Negro has received much from us, and has profited greatly therefrom; but all that he has received he has modified in accordance with his racial mental-set, and his psychical reactions to the influences of our civilization are entirely different from our own, and will necessarily remain so as long as the Negro is a Negro. No matter how much we educate him, no matter how much we better his position in society, he will remain a Negro psychically as long as he remains a Negro physically. We may cause him to absorb the full, rich store of our cultural elements, but by the time these elements have gone through the channels of his thought they will be profoundly modified, and they will take on a different meaning in the Negro's consciousness from what they have in the white man's consciousness. Concomitantly, these cultural elements will modify the brain of the Negro; but this modification will not follow the same pathways and will not give the same results as it would in the untutored brain, say, of a white child. The modifying forces acting upon the Negro's brain will have to start with an anatomical structure already formed and set by heredity, an anatomical structure different from that of the white race, which produced the modifying forces in question, and the final result in the Negro's brain will be determined and directed by this preexistent anatomical make-up. So that the brain and the consciousness resulting from the absorption of our culture by the Negroes will be a brain and a consciousness different from our own to the same extent that the Negro differs from us in other respects, and both will be characteristically Negroid in nature, not European.

It follows, therefore, that present ideals in regard to the "solution" of our Negro problems (ideals, as has been pointed out and which it is well to reiterate, resulting from the confusion of ethical and scientific principles) are biologically fallacious, and impossible of attainment. We can never make the Negro like the white man mentally. We can never have a bi-racial state based upon an identity of ideas and political philosophies in both races. . . .

This fact, rather than ethical theory, should form the foundation of American thought in regard to the Negroes and the Negro problem.

The Psychology of
Race Prejudice*

WILLIAM I. THOMAS

One of the cornerstones of segregationist thought is that race prejudice is not a "prejudice" but an instinct. Every normal individual, so the idea runs, has an inborn aversion for the strange and alien and a deep-seated "consciousness of kind," an instinctive identification with members of his own race. This is the elemental idea of scientific racism. It offers an ostensibly scientific explanation for racial antipathy, and coincidentally relieves the conscience of segregationists, telling them their racial views are innate rather than bigoted. It also places race policy beyond the moralist's reach, or that at least is the segregationists' conclusion. The idea was not the invention of segregationists. On the contrary, it was widely accepted by social scientists around the turn of the century, as the following article by sociologist William I. Thomas of the University of Chicago indicates. Thomas was a widely respected social scientist; his interest in the subject was that of a seeker of scientific truth. He had little interest in southern race policy and even less in rationalizing white supremacy. His article therefore illustrates the manner in which "disinterested" social scientists served the needs of calculating racists. It is typical of the vast body of "scientific" literature which segregationists could—and did—cite as evidence of the correctness of their racial policies.

In looking for an explanation of the antipathy which one race feels toward another, we may first of all inquire whether there are any conditions arising in the course of the biological development of a species which, aside from social activities, lead to a predilection for those of one's own kind and a prejudice against organically different

*Reprinted from William I. Thomas, "The Psychology of Race Prejudice," *American Journal of Sociology*, Vol. IX (March, 1904, pp. 593-611).

groups. And we do, in fact, find such conditions. The earliest movements of animal life involve, in the rejection of stimulations vitally bad, an attitude which is the analogue of prejudice. On the principle of chemiotaxis, the micro-organism will approach a particle of food placed in the water and shun a particle of poison; and its movements are similarly controlled by heat, light, electricity, and other tropic forces. The development of animal life from this point upward consists in the growth of structure and organs of sense adapted to discriminate between different stimulations, to choose between the beneficial and prejudicial, and to obtain in this way a more complete control of the environment. Passing over the lower forms of animal life, we find in the human type the power of attention, memory, and comparison highly developed, so that an estimate is put on stimulations and situations correspondent with the bearing of stimulations or situations of this type on welfare in the past. The choice and rejection involved in this process are accompanied by organic changes (felt as emotions) designed to assist in the action which follows a decision. Both the judgment and the emotions are thus involved on the presentation to the senses of a situation or object involving possible advantage or hurt, pleasure or pain. It consequently transpires that the feelings called out on the presentation of disagreeable objects and their contrary are very different, and there arise in this connection fixed mental attitudes corresponding with fixed or habitually recurrent external situations—hate and love, prejudice and predilection—answering to situations which revive feelings of pain on the one hand, and feelings of pleasure on the other. And such is the working of suggestion that not alone an object or situation may produce a given state of feeling, but a voice, an odor, a color, or any characteristic sign of an object may produce the same effect as the object itself. . . .

"Unaccommodated man" was, to begin with, in relations more hostile than friendly. The struggle for food was so serious a fact, and predaciousness to such a degree the habit of life, that a suspicious, hostile, and hateful state of mind was the rule, with exceptions only in the cases where truce, association, and alliance had come about in the course of experience. This was still the state of affairs in so advanced a stage of development as the Indian society of North America, where a tribe was in a state of war with every tribe with which it had not made a treaty of peace; and it is perhaps true, generally speaking, of men today, that they regard others with a degree of distrust and aversion until they have proved themselves good fellows.

What, indeed, would be the fate of a man on the streets of a city if he did otherwise? There has, nevertheless, grown up an intimate relation between man and certain portions of his environment, and this includes not only his wife and children, his dog and his blood-brother, but, with lessening intensity, the members of his clan, tribe, and nation. These become, psychologically speaking, a portion of himself, and stand with him against the world at large. From the standpoint here outlined, prejudice or its analogue is the starting-point, and our question becomes one of the determination of the steps of the process by which man mentally allied with himself certain portions of his environment to the exclusion [of] others.

When we come to examine in detail the process by which an associational and sympathetic relation is set up between the individual and certain parts of the outside world to the exclusion of others, we find this at first on a purely instinctive and reflex basis, originating in connection with food-getting and reproduction, and growing more conscious in the higher forms of life. One of the most important origins of association and prepossession is seen in the relation of parents, particularly of mothers, to children. This begins, of course, among the lower animals. The mammalian class, in particular, is distinguished by the strength and persistence of the devotion of parents to offspring. The advantage secured by the form of reproduction characteristic of man and the other mammals is that a closer connection is secured between the child and the mother. By the intra-uterine form of reproduction the association of mother and offspring is set up in an organic way before the birth of the latter, and is continued and put on a social basis during the period of lactation and the early helpless years of the child. By continuing the helpless period of the young for a period of years, nature has made provision on the time side for a complex physical and mental type, impossible in types thrown at birth on their own resources. . . . In the course of development every variational tendency in mothers to dote on their children was rewarded by the survival of these children, and the consequent survival of the stock, owing to better nutrition, protection, and training. . . .

This interest and providence on the score of offspring has also a characteristic expression on the mental side. All sense-perceptions are colored and all judgments biased where the child is in question, and affection for it extends to the particular marks which distinguish it. Not only its physical features, but its dress and little shoes, its toys and everything it has touched, take on a peculiar aspect. This tendency of the attention and memory to seize on characteristic aspects, and to be obsessed by them to the exclusion or disparagement of contrasted aspects is an important condition in the psychology of race-prejudice. It implies a set of conditions in which the attention is practiced in attaching peculiar values to signs of personality—conditions differing also from those arising in the reaction to environment on the food side.

Another origin of a sympathetic attitude toward those of our own kind is seen in connection with courtship. As a result of selection, doubtless, there is a peculiar organic response on the part of either sex to the presence and peculiarities of the other. Among birds the voice, plumage, odor, ornamentation, and movements of the male are in the wooing season powerful excitants to the female. These aspects of the male, which are the most conspicuous of his characteristics, are recognized as the marks of maleness by the female, and she is most deeply impressed, and is in fact won, by the male most conspicuously marked and displaying these marks most skilfully. And in the same way feminine traits and behavior exercise a powerful influence on the male. It is of particular significance just here that the attention is able to single out particular marks of the personality of the opposite sex, and that these marks become the carriers of the whole fund of sexual suggestion. This interest in the characteristic features of the opposite sex has always dominated fashion and ornament to a large extent in human society, and this is particularly true in historical times in connection with women, who are both the objects of sexual attention and the exponents of fashion. The white lady uses face powder and rouge to emphasize her white-and-pink complexion, and the African lady uses charcoal and fat to enhance the luster of her ebony skin. . . .

In still another connection, that of co-operative activity, there is a tendency to knit alliances with others; and here also the attention shows the tendency to fix on characteristic signs and attach emotional values to them. It was pointed out above that the first efforts of the animal to adjust itself to its food environment were on a purely chemical and physical basis, and we find that its first movements toward a combination with other organisms in an associational relation are equally unreflective. . . .

Among mammalian forms, . . . an instinctive, if not reflective, appreciation of the presence and personality of others is seen in the fact of gregariousness, and here already a definite meaning is attached to signs of personality. In fact, a certain grade of memory is all that is essential to antipathy or affection. In mankind various practices show a growing "consciousness of kind," there is resort to symbolism to secure and increase the feeling of solidarity, and finally a dependence of emotional states on this symbolism. . . .

Tribal marks are another widespread sign of consciousness of community of interest. Sacrification, tattooing, bodily mutilations, totemic marks, and other devices of this nature are consciously and unconsciously employed to keep up the feeling of group solidarity; and whether instituted with this end in view or not, any visible marks which become by usage characteristic of the group represent to the group-mind the associational and emotional past of the group. A similar dependence of cultural groups on signs of solidarity is seen in the enthusiasm aroused by the display of the flag of our country or the playing of a national air.

Habit also plays an important role in our emotional attitude toward the unfamiliar. The usual is felt as comfortable and safe, and a sinister view is taken of the unknown. When things are running along habitual lines, the attention is relaxed and the emotional processes are running low. A disturbance of habit throws a strain on the attention, and the emotional processes are accelerated in the attempt to accommodate. And since the normal attitude, as noted above, is one of distrust toward everything not included in the old run of habits, we find the most sinister meaning attached to signs of unfamiliar personality. . . .

By some such steps as we have outlined a group whose members have a history in common has to some degree a consciousness in common, and common emotional reactions. . . .

If it is assumed, then, that the group comes to have a quasi-personality, and that, like the individual, it is in an attitude of suspicion and hostility toward the outside world, and that, like the individual also, it has a feeling of intimacy with itself, it follows that the signs of unlikeness in another group are regarded with prejudice. It is also a characteristic of the attention that unlikeness is determined by the aid of certain external signs—namely, physical features, dress, speech, social habits, etc.—and that the concrete expressions of prejudice are seen in connection with these. . . .

Race prejudice is in one sense a superficial matter. It is called out primarily by the physical aspect of an unfamiliar people—their color, form and feature, and dress—and by their activities and habits in only a secondary way. The general organic attitude, growing out of experience (through reflex rather than deliberative experience), is that the outside world is antagonistic and subject to depredation, and this attitude seems to be localized in a prejudice felt for the characteristic appearance of others, this being most apprehensible by the senses. This prejudice is intense and immediate, sharing in this respect the character of the instinctive reactions in general. It cannot be reasoned with, because, like the other instincts, it originated before deliberative brain centers were developed, and is not to any great extent under their control. Like the other instincts also, it has a persistence and a certain automatism appropriate to a type of reaction valuable in the organic scheme, but not under the control of the deliberative centers. But for all its intensity, race-prejudice, like the other instinctive movements, is easily dissipated or converted into its opposite by association, or a slight modification of stimulus. . . .

The negro for his part, not only loses race-prejudice in the presence of the white man, but repudiates black standards.[1] In America the papers printed for black readers contain advertisements of pomades for making kinky hair straight and of washes to change the Ethiopian's skin; and the slaves returning to Sierra Leone in 1820 assumed the role of whites, even referred to themselves [as] white, and called the natives "bush niggers." . . .

When not complicated with caste-feeling, race-prejudice is, after all, very impermanent, of no more stability, perhaps, than fashions.[2] . . . Psychologically speaking, race-prejudice and caste feeling are at bottom the same thing, both being phases of the instinct of hate, but a status of caste is reached as the result of competitive activities. The lower caste has either been conquered and captured, or gradually outstripped on account of the mental and economic inferiority. Under these conditions, it is psychologically important to the higher

---

[1]This statement illustrates the difficulty segregationists encountered in their effort to make race prejudice and "consciousness of kind" into instinctive qualities: whites generally seem more "conscious" of their kind and more prejudiced than Negroes. Thomas is saying in this paragraph that the American environment has in effect neutralized an instinct. Incidentally, the implications of an instinctive consciousness of kind for mulattoes are fascinating.

[2]Such statements as these indicate Thomas' ambivalence on the subject of innate race prejudice. If racial prejudice shares "the character of instinctive reactions in general," as he wrote earlier, it seems illogical that it might on occasion be as "impermanent" as fashions. This ambivalence was perhaps a result of Thomas' unwillingness to accept the pessimistic implications of his own ideas. If race prejudice is instinctive, nothing can be done about it; it cannot be eliminated, or hardly even neutralized.

caste to maintain the feeling and show of superiority, on account of the suggestive effect of this on both the inferior caste and on itself; and signs of superiority and inferiority, being thus aids to the manipulation of one class by another, acquire a new significance and become more ineradicable. Of the relation of black to white in this country it is perhaps true that the antipathy of the southerner for the negro is rather caste-feeling than race-prejudice, while the feeling of the northerner is race-prejudice proper. In the North, where there has been no contact with the negro and no activity connections, there is no caste-feeling, but there exists a sort of *skin*-prejudice—a horror of the external aspect of the negro—and many northerners report that they have a feeling against eating from a dish handled by a negro. The association of master and slave in the South was, however, close, even if not intimate, and much of the feeling of physical repulsion for a black skin disappeared. This was particularly true of the house servants. White girls and boys kissed their black mammies with real affection, and after marriage returned from other states to the funeral of an old slave. But while color was not here repulsive, it was so ineradicably associated with inferiority that it was impossible for a southern white to think the negro into his own class. . . .

Race-prejudice is an instinct originating in the tribal stage of society, when solidarity in feeling and action were essential to the preservation of the group. It, or some analogue of it, will probably never disappear completely, since an identity of standards, traditions, and physical appearance in all geographical zones is neither possible nor aesthetically desirable. It is, too, an affair which can neither be reasoned with nor legislated about very effectively, because it is connected with the affective, rather than the cognitive, processes. . . .

Legislation Cannot
Make Mores*

WILLIAM GRAHAM SUMNER

If race prejudice is instinctive (as Professor Thomas asserted in the previous article), that fact has profound implications for racial policy. Policies which ignore such a fact of human nature can only be forced and artificial, and doomed to failure. This idea, widely held in the late 19th and early 20th centuries, is still a basic element of segregationist thought. It is rooted in a larger belief: that all social mores are ultimately rooted in those instincts and urges which comprise human nature, and are beyond the manipulation of environmentalists and reformers. In William Graham Sumner's words, "legislation cannot make mores." In view of the widespread acceptance of this idea by segregationists, it is ironic that segregation itself wrought a new matrix of racial mores, and was itself in part the product of legislation and coercion. In the following brief excerpt, Sumner, a Yale sociologist and political economist and perhaps the nation's foremost social Darwinist, applies his ideas about the immutability of folkways to race relations in the South.

In our southern states, before the civil war, whites and blacks had formed habits of action and feeling towards each other. They lived in peace and concord, and each one grew up in the ways which were traditional and customary. The civil war abolished legal rights and left the two races to learn how to live together under other relations than before. The whites have never been converted from the old mores. Those who still survive look back with regret and affection to the old social usages and customary sentiments and feelings. The two races have not yet made new mores. Vain attempts have been made

*Reprinted from William Graham Sumner, *Folkways* (New York: Ginn & Co., 1906), pp. 77-78.

to control the new order by legislation. The only result is the proof that legislation cannot make mores. We see also that mores do not form under social convulsion and discord. It is only just now that the new society seems to be taking shape. There is a trend in the mores now as they begin to form under the new state of things. It is not at all what the humanitarians hoped and expected. The two races are separating more than ever before. The strongest point in the new code seems to be that any white man is boycotted and despised if he "associates with negroes". . . . Some are anxious to interfere and try to control. They take their stand on ethical views of what is going on. It is evidently impossible for any one to interfere. We are like spectators at a great natural convulsion. The results will be such as the facts and forces call for. We cannot foresee them. They do not depend on ethical views any more than the volcanic eruption on Martinique contained an ethical element. All the faiths, hopes, energies, and sacrifices of both whites and blacks are components in the new construction of folkways by which the two races will learn how to live together. As we go along with the constructive process it is very plain that what once was, or what any one thinks ought to be, but slightly affects what, at any moment, is. The mores which once were are a memory. Those which any one thinks ought to be are a dream. The only thing with which we can deal are those which are. . . .

The humanitarians of the nineteenth century did not settle anything. The contact of two races and two civilizations cannot be settled by any dogma. Evidence is presented every day that the problems are not settled and cannot be settled by dogmatic and sentimental generalities.

The Negro Brain*

ROBERT BENNETT BEAN

Prior to World War I, scientists and social scientists produced a flood of literature which purported to demonstrate racial inequality and Negro inferiority. Inequality, they believed, was mental as well as physical, and mental inequalities have a physiological base. Now, the most important organ in the human body is the brain, and if Negroes are inferior to whites it necessarily follows that that "fact" will be reflected in the brains of the two races. Negro brains, in other words, must be demonstrably inferior to Caucasian brains. In the following article, Professor (of anatomy) Robert Bennett Bean, an M.D., of the University of Virginia, describes the alleged inferiority of Negro brains, and notes the implications that "fact" has for racial policy. This article is a popularized version of the study Bean reported in "Some Racial Peculiarities of the Negro Brain," American Journal of Anatomy, *Vol. V (September, 1906), pp. 353-432. It illustrates the scientific deficiencies characteristic of most of the literature of scientific racism, especially the author's willingness to use his "scientific" data as a basis for racist sociology. Despite the limitations of Bean's study, the views expressed in it have been commonly held by segregationists throughout the 20th century.*

. . . In the ultimate settlement of this imminently critical [race] question the facts of scientific investigation should not be ignored. Not only should an earnest philanthropy and an honest statesmanship be brought to the solution of the negro problem, but the fundamental physical and mental differences of the white and black races should be considered in any rational adjustment of the relations between them, and a just discrimination of the character and genius of each race should be made.

It is an undoubted fact that environment affects the individual

*Reprinted from Robert Bennett Bean, "The Negro Brain," *Century Magazine*, Vol. LXXII (October, 1906), pp. 778-84.

more than the race, whereas heredity affects the race more than the individual. Individuals may be altered without altering the race. By both heredity and environment we may explain the greatness of certain men like [Alexander] Dumas, Booker Washington, [Bishop Benjamin T.] Tanner, and Professor [W. E. B.] Dubois, who are classed as negroes, but are not pure negroes ethnically. . . .

The subject in all its phases cannot be considered here, but the attention of the reader may be directed to one or two significant facts. The first is that the negro race is now considered to be one of the oldest races in the world, evidences of its existence in prehistoric times having been recently discovered throughout Africa, Australia, and Oceania. In historic times negroes are depicted on the monuments of Egypt thousands of years before the Anglo-Saxon had emerged from barbarism. They have been in contact continually with the highest civilizations of antiquity, but have never risen to the eminence of other nations, having retained their primitive condition, even as is now apparent in the Southern States, where they are isolated in large masses.

Another significant fact is that the negro brain is smaller than the Caucasian, the difference in size being represented in both gray matter (nerve cells) and white matter (nerve fibers), as I will attempt presently to demonstrate. Brain cells are the basis of brain power or mental ability, and their number is known to remain constant throughout life, so that there seems never to be a degree of mental development beyond the possible expression of the brain cells inherited. Development of mental activity by experience, education, etc., is considered to be correlated with the development of sheaths around the nerve fibers as they become active in the transmission of impulses. The efficiency of the brain depends upon the number and position of such nerve fibers, just as the efficiency of a telephone system depends upon the number of its various connections and ramifications. The negro brain having fewer nerve cells and nerve fibers, assuming that gray matter and white matter respectively represent these numerically, the possibilities of developing the negro are therefore limited, except by crossing with other races. This has been done to such an extent in times past that it is difficult to determine whether a pure negro really exists in America. . . .

[My discussion] of the American negro is based upon an intimate study at close range of thousands of individuals in various parts of the South and the North, and it has been confirmed by the careful inspection and measurement of one hundred and three brains, individuals of the various classes presenting, according to my observations, recognizable differences in their brain development.[1] I do not purpose to enter into a discussion of these differences here, but desire to consider the larger questions as to differences of brain development in the negro and the white as demonstrated by a comparison of the negro brains mentioned above with forty-nine brains of American Caucasians. The brains I studied were accurately weighed, and the weights are classified as follows:

Average weight of 51 Caucasian male brains	1,341 grams
" " " 9 " female "	1,103 "
" " " 51 negro male "	1,292 "
" " " 28 " female "	1,108 "

These brains were from a representative element of the American negro population, and from the lower classes of the whites, especially the white females, which are from a notably low social class. The brain of the negro male is demonstrably smaller than that of the Caucasian male. The brains from the females of the two races are virtually the same size. The brain weights of thirty-two negro brains collected from various sources in going over the literature of the subject are given here. The average weight of twenty-two male negro brains, weighed by sundry men, at various times, in divers places, with different systems and under dissimilar conditions, is 1,256 grams. The average weight of ten female negro brains of a like assortment is 980 grams. Waldeyer, a German anatomist, gives the average weight of twelve negro brains in the fresh state as 1,148 grams. These are European records, the brains being obtained from native tribes of Africa and elsewhere. It is evident that the brain of the American negro weighs more than the native African, which is no doubt because of the greater amount of white blood in the American negro. Sandford B. Hunt, M.D., and surgeon Ira Russel, of the 11th Massachusetts Volunteers (Civil War), represent by an ethnological table (part of which is reproduced below) that the weight of the brain in

---

[1]Except among segregationists, Bean's study of Negro brains is today considered worthless. For a recent criticism of it, see Dwight J. Ingle, "Comments on the Teachings of Carleton Putnam," *Mankind Quarterly*, Vol. IV (1963), pp. 28-48. Ingle is a professor of physiology at the University of Chicago and editor of *Perspectives in Biology and Medicine*. He found Bean's methodology unscientific and his conclusions invalid. "The presently existing evidence for inferiority of the Negro brain is without value," he wrote. "It has not been possible to prove a genetic basis for racial differences in achievement, drives and aptitude." *Ibid.*, p. 40.

the American negro varies directly in proportion to the amount of white blood in the individual, those less than one half white having smaller brains than the pure negro. To this table are added the results of a similar classification of the brains weighed by me.

ETHNOLOGICAL. ALL MALES

Number of Brains	Grade of Color	Average Brain Weight		Number of Brains
		H & R	Bean	
24	White	1478 grams	1341 grams	51
25	3/4 "	1390 "	–	–
47	1/2 "	1331 "	1347 "	3
51	1/4 "	1315 "	1340 "	15
95	1/8 "	1305 "	1235 "	16
22	1/10 "	1275 "	1191 "	10
141	Black	1328 "	1157 "	7

The brain weights of more than 4000 individuals of various Caucasian nationalities collected by Marshall of England, Retzius of Sweden, Bischoff and Marchand of Germany, Matieka of Bohemia (Slavs), and others, show an average of about 1400 grams for males and about 1250 grams for females. . . . It is evident, then, that the Caucasian brain is larger than the negro brain, and the above table demonstrates that in a mixture of the races the brain weight resulting is directly in proportion to the amount of Caucasian blood in the individual, other things being equal. The body weight and stature are in intimate relation to brain weight, intellectual ability is one of the components of brain weight, but sexual as well as racial relations are evident, so that brain weight is not a safe criterion of intelligence.

The size and weight of the brain, however, are not the only differences determined. The size and shape of the front end of the brain is [sic] different in the two races, being smaller and more angular in the negro, while it is larger and more rounded in the Caucasian. . . . Vertical sections taken through the frontal lobes [are] between 1.5 and 2 centimeters from the front end of the brain of a negro, and between 2 and 2.5 centimeters from the front end of the brain of a Caucasian. The section of the Caucasian brain is larger, and more nearly circular than that of the negro, not exhibiting the narrow projecting sides, and pointed tips above and below, such as are seen on the negro brain. The convolutions of the Caucasian brain are more elaborate, and the fissures are deeper, than in the negro brain, while the relative amount of white matter is greater in the Caucasian brain. . . .

[A diagramatic illustration shows] the more rounded outline of the Caucasian brain and the squarer outline of the negro brain with the flat side toward the front end, this being eminently characteristic of the brain of the negro. This flat surface indicates a smaller anterior association area in the negro brain.

The racial difference is not only evident when looking at the brains, or drawings made from them, but can be demonstrated by actual measurements made from the middle point of each brain to a point over the middle of each association area, anterior and posterior. . . . The results of such measurements are given in averages in the following table:

Race–Sex	Number of Brains	From Middle of Brain to Middle of Anterior Assoc'n Area	From Middle of Brain to Middle of Posterior Assoc'n Area	Ratio
Caucasian male. . .	34	70 mm.	72 mm.	97-100
Negro male	43	66 mm.	74 mm.	89-100
Caucasian female .	8	65 mm.	67 mm.	97-100
Negro female . . .	22	62 mm.	68 mm.	89-100

This difference is manifested not only in the apparent size of the anterior association area thus obtained, but also in its more intimate structure. The two ends of the corpus callosum, the great band of fibers that connects the two hemispheres of the brain, and associates the functions of the two sides of the brain, exhibit the same difference in a more marked way. In separating the two hemispheres, this band of fibers is cut squarely across, so that, by measuring the areas of the front and hind ends of this cut surface, one obtains an accurate representation of the size of the connecting link between the front and hind ends of the brain. The cross section area of the two ends of the corpus callosum being accurately measured, the results are given in averages.

Race–Sex	No. of Brains	Front End	Hind End	Ratio
Caucasian male.	42	3.70 sq.cm.	3.04 sq.cm.	122-100
Negro male	62	3.07 sq.cm.	3.02 sq.cm.	102-100
Caucasian female . . .	9	3.17 sq.cm.	2.87 sq.cm.	110-100
Negro female	25	2.86 sq.cm.	2.86 sq.cm.	100-100

This suggests a probable difference in the relative power, or capacity, or activity, of the frontal lobes in the brains of the two races, there being a difference of 20% in favor of the Caucasian. This is much greater in many individuals.

Having established the facts (1) that the Caucasian brain is heavier than that of the negro, (2) that the relative quantity of the white fiber is greater in the Caucasian than in the negro, and (3) that the anterior association center (front end of the brain) and the front end of the corpus callosum are larger in the Caucasian than in the negro, let us consider their significance. The first two propositions corroborate the statement made previously, that the negro brain contains less gray matter (nerve cells) and white matter (nerve fibers) than the Caucasian. Dismissing this, then, let us consider the third proposition.

In the discussion of this proposition the word "subjective" is used in the sense of rational, and is related to judgment and reason, or the abstract qualities, whereas the word "objective" is used in the sense of perception, or the processes of reflex phenomena, or of association, meaning perception in the concrete. The known centers in the brain will be located according to function, then they will be discussed in relation to the facts just established. In the hind part of the brain are located the areas for sight, hearing, taste, and smell, and the body sense area that receives impressions from the whole surface of the body, from the muscles, and from the viscera. Besides this, in the midst of these areas, there is a large region called the posterior association area. The posterior association area is intimately connected with the special sense areas, just mentioned, and is considered to represent the objective faculties.

In the front part of the brain are located the motor area, part of the area for smell, and the great anterior association area. This association area is closely connected with the area that controls the muscles of the body, and contains definite bands of fibers to all other areas of the brain, and is connected with the lower centers of the nervous system. It represents the subjective faculties, the great reasoning center, the center for abstract thought. Lesions of the anterior association area are known to cause alteration or loss of ideas regarding personality; the subjective self; a loss of self-control, of the powers of inhibition, of will power; a diminution in the capacity for ethical and esthetic judgment. In simple lesions, or in the early stages of the lesion, when the person is "subjected to unaccounted stimuli, especially to sexual excitement, anger, or vexation, he may lose all control of his movements and acts, so that simple influence may lead him to try to satisfy his desire without any regard to custom or good taste. In late stages of the disease imbecility may appear, with entire loss of the mental pictures regarding personality." The individual may distort his own personality, and be unable to distinguish the imagined from the real: thus he may think himself of enormous dignity, of great importance, or that he is possessed of great wealth, or that he is a genius. The anterior association area in the front end of the brain, then, represents the "ego," the subjective self, the personality, orientation. Here probably reside the highest developed faculties of man, the motor speech-center for the command of language; will power, the power of self-control, the power of inhibition and perseverance; the ethical and esthetic faculties; and the power of thought in the abstract. The posterior association area in the hind part of the brain, on the other hand, represents the special senses—the appetites of man, sensuality, the passions. Here probably reside the artistic sense, the musical sense, the objective faculties, and the power of perception in the concrete. The anterior association area probably controls or directs the powers of the posterior association area. In the Caucasian the anterior association area is larger and better developed than in the negro. The posterior association area is about the same size in the two races. Let us see, then, if the known characteristics of the Caucasian and negro coincide with the relations of their brains.

The Caucasian has the subjective faculties well developed; the negro, the objective. The Caucasian, and more particularly the Anglo-Saxon, is dominant and domineering, and possessed primarily with determination, will power, self-control, self-government, and all the attributes of the subjective self, with a high development of the ethical and esthetic faculties and great reasoning powers. The negro is in direct contrast by reason of a certain lack of these powers, and a great development of the objective qualities. The negro is primarily affectionate, immensely emotional, then sensual, and under provocation, passionate. There is love of outward show, of ostentation, of approbation. He loves melody and a rude kind of poetry and sonorous language. There is undeveloped artistic power and taste—negroes make good artisans and handicraftsmen. They are deficient in judgment, in the formulation of new ideas from existing facts, in devising hypotheses, and in making deductions in general. They are imitative rather than original, inventive, or constructive. There is instability of character incident to lack of self-control, especially in connection with the sexual relation, and there is a lack of orientation, or recognition of position and condition of self and environment, evidenced in various ways, but by a peculiar "bumptiousness," so called by Prof. Blackshear of Texas, this is particularly noticeable.

The white and the black races are antipodal, then, in cardinal points. The one has a large frontal region of the brain, the other a larger region behind; the one is subjective, the other objective; the one a great reasoner, the other preeminently emotional; the one domineering, but having great self-control, the other meek and submissive, but violent and lacking self-control when the passions are aroused; the one a very advanced race, the other a very backward one. The Caucasian and the negro are fundamentally opposite extremes in evolution.

Having demonstrated that the negro and the Caucasian are widely different in characteristics, due to a deficiency of gray matter and connecting fibers in the negro brain, especially in the frontal lobes, a deficiency that is hereditary and can be altered only by intermarriage, we are forced to conclude that it is useless to try to elevate the negro by education or otherwise, except in the direction of his natural endowments. The way may be made plain to the black people, and they may be encouraged in the proper direction, but the solution of the question still must come from within the race. Let them win their reward by diligent service.

The Permanence of Racial Characteristics*

NATHANIEL SOUTHGATE SHALER

Scientists such as Dr. Bean "proved" that Negroes are inferior to whites. Other scientists were concerned to point out that this alleged inferiority is inherited from generation to generation. The two decades after 1890 not only witnessed the institutionalization of segregation and disfranchisement in the South but also evidenced a profound interest in the new science of heredity. The new science, however, contained more novelty than science. A victim of the over-enthusiasm of youth, it fell an easy prey to racists and segregationists. By 1910 eugenics had achieved the proportions of a national fad and was often applied to Negroes and the "Negro problem." The Negro "lacks in his germ-plasm excellence of some qualities which the white races possess, and which are essential for success" in modern civilization, wrote two prominent geneticists in 1918. Consequently, "if eugenics is to be thought of solely in terms of the white race, there can be no hesitation about rendering a verdict. We must unhesitatingly condemn miscegenation."[1] Many scientists and social scientists who endorsed these views thought of themselves as disinterested men of science. Others combined the scientific spirit with traditional southern paternalism and used science to bolster Southern race policies. One of the latter group was Nathaniel Southgate Shaler, the son of a Kentucky slaveholder who rose to become head of Harvard's Lawrence Scientific School. A prolific writer on the subject of racial and ethnic relations, Professor Shaler was dedicated to both scientific

---

*Reprinted from N. S. Shaler, "The Nature of the Negro," *Arena,* Vol. III (December, 1890), pp. 23-35.

[1]Paul Popenoe and Roswell Hill Johnson, *Applied Eugenics* (New York: Macmillan, 1918), pp. 285, 292.

truth and Negro uplift. In the following excerpts, written for a popular journal, he discusses the racial characteristics of American Negroes, emphasizing their innate, inherited nature. But then, paradoxically, he suggests they may be altered for the better by paternal racial policies.

Men of science have at length found a clue to unravel a part of the mysteries which surround the matter of human relations[.] The knowledge of the laws of inheritance, one of the affirmed triumphs of modern biology, has led us to understand the extent to which the conduct of men is determined by the habits of their ancestors.

This view of the conditions of the human quality is novel only in the measure of affirmation which modern knowledge has given it. . . . Science has only fathomed the deeps of which the surface was well known in common experience. The Hebrew bible and all similar harvests of knowledge is [sic] full of these ideas as to the fixedness of racial attributes. Investigators have only extended the conception by showing that the varieties of men, following a common original law, hold fast to the ways of their forefathers, and that the moral as well as the physical characteristics of a race are to a greater or less degree indelible, whether the given kind belong to the human or to lower creatures. It is evident that this well affirmed theory is of the utmost importance to us when we have to consider the nature of any people [i.e., Negro Americans] who have been placed in [a new environment]. If we trust to this view as all naturalists do, the first object of our inquiry should be to trace as far as we may, the origin and nurture of the race which is the object of our inquiry; to see what their historic environment has been; and to ascertain the peculiarities which their habits of life have bred in them. . . .

The negroes[2] of this country were derived from truly tropical folk. No other population in the world seems to have been so long under the influence of the vertical sun. Although there is a considerable and, as we may see hereafter, a very important difference in the nature of their origin as regards the quality of their ancestors, they are all deeply and apparently indelibly stamped with the mark of

---

[2]This and the following paragraph are excerpted from a somewhat earlier article by Professor Shaler, "The African Element in America," *Arena*, Vol. II (November, 1890), pp. 664-65.

their long-continued residence in equatorial lands. Such climatal and other environing conditions produce peculiar types of men; they tend, indeed, to bring the most diverse races into something like the same moral and intellectual state. It is not easy for those who have been bred in high latitudes [i.e., Caucasians] to conceive the way in which Nature effects [sic] the equatorial races; the northern winter rather than the summer of the Aryan lands has shaped their motives. The struggle with a rude Nature which our ancestors have endured in the ages while their race characteristics were making, has been one long war with winter's trials. In the battle they have learned thrift, the habit of continuous labor, the consummate art of sparing the moment's pleasure for the profit of to-morrow. They have had to store the products of their toil and to interchange them with the fruits of other lands, for no one field of their tilling can produce all the materials which they need. The indolent and the shiftless have been constantly taken away by the death which speedily comes to the weak beneath the cruel testing of a northern sky.

It is very different with the intertropical man; there the nearly uniform temperature takes away the need of much clothing, and makes artificial heat unnecessary save for cooking food. Such food as the fields or wilderness afford, is generally to be had at all times of the year, or if there be harvests they come repeatedly and demand little husbanding. A thatch is sufficient shelter and a wall of thorns a stronghold. Although the tropics have their trials, their lands are, in their physical and moral effects, like an almshouse where men are disciplined to inaction and deprived of all the educative influence of evitable dangers. . . . It was in these lands of enduring ease that our African people were cradled, while our savage and barbarian ancestors were combatting the winters in the stubborn fields of the high North, and receiving thereby the precious heritage of energy and foresight which has given them the mastery of the world. . . .

[An examination of the characteristics of Africans today will illustrate the racial qualities of American Negroes, qualities which our racial policies must take cognizance of.] The type of the Central African races [from which the greater part of American Negroes are derived] is very provincial, it is distinct from that of other peoples, and is therefore almost necessarily ancient, for it is almost an axiom with naturalists that well isolated organic forms have a relatively great antiquity. Moreover, the negro type of to-day is almost certainly nearer to the anthropoid or pre-human ancestry of men than the other marked varieties of our species, such as the Aryan, Tartars, or Semitic folk.[3] The measure of this approach to the lower beings whence men came, is less great than it is commonly assumed to be, but the closer affiliation seems clear. This also supports the presumption that the negro has been much longer in about the state in which we now find him than is the case with these other races of men. . . .

The conditions of these African tribes of today is that which characterizes all people who have taken the first relatively easy step above the lowest savagery and show no clear signs of ability to climb the next round of the ladder. They have learned a number of the earlier lessons of deliberate associated action and in so far are lifted above the level of the least advanced men, such as the Andaman islanders or the Bushmen. They have acquired the habit of subjection to chiefs, of the chase, of rude war, and of simple husbandry. As yet there are no conceptions of formal law, no organized commerce, no trace of any education of youth, no beginnings of the literary motive. Religion, save that derived from the foreign sources, is in the most primitive form of nature worship in which men have conceived of the forces which can do them ill, but have in no way organized this vague conception.

The moral status of these people is exceedingly primitive. While they are less cruel than most men of their general conditions, the sympathies are not much developed; they are limited to a moderate devotion to the chief in which fear plays the largest part; and to a love of their children. Friendship between equals, which is the flower of a higher civilization, is unknown. All the negroid races are rudely polygamous, and the wife has not risen above the grade of a chattel. The result is that there are no enduring families with their store of traditional pride, which has done so much to promote the advance of the races where marriage has a higher form. The general tone of the people is shown by the fact that cannibalism is rather common among them. . . . [This fact is of] value to us in our inquiry only for the reason that it shows how near the negro of Africa is in his motives to the elementary man. It would of itself suffice to show that a large part of the spiritual advance which forms the very foundation of

---

[3]This idea has been widely believed by racists and segregationists. It is a logical extension of their belief in racial inequality. The "evidence" for it is that certain of the Negro's physical characteristics are more "anthropoid" than those of whites; for example, the cephalic index. Of course it can also be said that many of the Caucasian's physical features are more "anthropoid" than those of Negroes; for example, hair texture, the distribution of body hair, facial configurations, and skin color.

civilization which, indeed, separates it from savagery, had not been won by these children of the dark continent when they gave their unwilling colonists to the new world. . . .

Their simple yet strongly inherited motives remained with [the African slaves brought to America], undergoing such changes of adjustment, not in nature, as the exigencies demanded. The uncomplicated social framework of slavery made it easier for the blacks to accommodate their ancient habits to the new life, than we might at first suppose would have been the case. The master took the place of the chief, to whom the black for immemorial ages had been accustomed to render the obedience and loyalty which fear inspires; under this white lord's control, he was hardly more a slave than before. On the whole this lowly man gained by the change in the quality of the servitude: by the contact with the new master he gradually acquired some sense of the motives of the dominant race. Christianity was imposed upon him by the superior will; at first he secured little save its external forms, but gradually some parts of this persuasive religion entered his mind and enlarged his conceptions of spiritual things. The discipline of orderly, associative labor, though the field of the activities was limited, had a civilizing influence, for it tended to subjugate the passions of the savage, and to make him more of the routine man which civilization demands.

The effect of the external manners of the dominant race has also had a great influence on the negro. While the bearing of a people is naturally the revelation of their inner motives, the external action when imitated, tends in a way to arouse the impulses which the action expresses. The negro is a very imitative creature; in no other feature does he so well show the strong, sympathetic quality of his nature; in this apeing of his social superiors, he has greatly helped his advance. . . . The negro is contented only when he feels that he has brought himself into accord with his superiors. . . .

Another important influence came to the blacks through their contact with the English language. The peculiar richness of this speech, the call it institutes upon the mind for contextual thoughts makes it to the savage perhaps the most educative of tongues. It cannot be compassed by any lowly people without a decidedly developing effect. The negro has mastered this language in a very remarkable manner, and without deliberate instruction by any form of schooling, and by so doing has given better proof of his natural capacity than by any other of his accomplishments in this to him very new world. . . .

The struggle of the African with the difficulties of our incompleted, open-structured English speech is one of the most interesting features of his history. His inherited habits of mind framed on a very limited language, where the terms were well tied together and where the thought found in the words a bridge of easy passage, gave him much trouble when he came to employ our speech where the words are like widely separated stepping-stones which require nimble wits in those who use them.[4] It would require a separate essay to deal with this interesting subject, so I can only note a few of the most instructive examples of the devices to which the negroes have resorted in their difficult task. . . . Our verb with its imperfect denotation of time and number gives them at first much trouble; to help themselves they have adopted some new but imperfectly defined tenses; "gwine done," "gone done," "done gone," seem to me to be natural efforts to give clearness to our indices of action, which we are able to supply from our grasp of the context,—a mental habit to which the lower races with difficulty attain. . . .

[Whereas West Indian Negroes often revolted against their masters] the negroes of the South [even during the Civil War] remained as peaceful and law abiding as did the poor whites. I have yet to learn of the slightest beginnings of armed revolt among them. Their own masters trusted them entirely, leaving to their care the helpless women and children with no fear as to the treatment which they would receive at their hands.

The riddle of the singular difference between the conduct of the West Indian slaves and those of our own country is, it seems to me, tolerably easy to read. The slaves of St. Domingo and Hayti, were largely new comers from Africa; they had, probably on the average,

---

[4]On the relationship between race and language, psychologist Anna Tolman Smith wrote in 1897 as follows: "Speech is a power that comes to most of us unconsciously, and the first stages of reading require little more than the visual recognition of signs that stand for familiar things. But, this stage passed, every word is a generalization, back of which lie traditions, customs, experiences, sentiments, and ideas, which are the heritage of a race. They are the stuff of the mind transmitted from generation to generation through the myriad channels of family, of social, of school, of church, and of business life. It is obvious that to a race wanting in our own experiences a large part of our vocabulary must be meaningless. Analogous experiences, of course, give insight into a foreign tongue, but here the colored child is at a peculiar disadvantage. The traditions of African savagery, even if they had reached him, offer no likeness to the history of the Anglo-Saxon. Slavery was a state with laws and customs and ceremonies bearing certain resemblances to our own, but the negro who has passed from this state to the freedom of American citizenship is, as it were, a man without ancestral history." Anna Tolman Smith, "A Study in Race Psychology," *Popular Science Monthly*, Vol. L (January-March, 1897), pp. 359-60.

not been for more than one generation in their pupilage as slaves; the greater part of them were plantation hands who had little or no contact with the superior race. Moreover, their masters were of a lower moral and intellectual grade than those who held the slaves of the southern States. Our African people had probably been in their new educative conditions on the average for four or five generations; during this time they had generally been domesticated with their masters. . . . Moreover, their masters were of the race which has the capacity of dominating alien people, and impressing them with its motives in a way possessed by none others. The schooling of the negro in the households of the South, was such as no savages had ever received from a superior race; it is unlikely that a lowly people will ever again secure such effective training. . . .

In considering the directions in which the negro has advanced during his life in this country, we must note the fact that he has mainly gained by the growth of those virtues, the seeds of which were planted in his African experience. Respect for authority, however it came to be set over him, laboriousness above the level of common savages, a kindly humor, were all native in him, and have been merely extended by his American training. His gentleness and decency of conduct are the principal moral gains which he has made. The intellectual advance which he has acquired is hardly to be measured, but it is evidently great; there are hundreds, if not thousands, of black men in this country who in capacity are to be ranked with the superior persons of the dominant race. And it is hard to say that in any evident feature of mind they characteristically differ from their white fellow citizens. Good, however, as is this record of advance, there are many and exceeding difficulties which the negro has to overcome before he can claim a permanent place in the civilization with which it has been his good fortune to come in contact. We must now consider this part of the problem.

It seems to me that the greatest difficulty with the negro in his present state of social development arises from his inability to combine his work with that of other men. This feature is well shown by the almost entire absence of partnership relations between them. I have never been able to find a trustworthy instance in which the black man of the pure race had entered on this relation which is almost the foundation of our modern business life. So far as I have been able to learn, this form of economic association, though perhaps not coeval with civilization, is yet very old, and the lack of it among the negroes probably indicates the absence of confidence in their neighbors which is characteristic of primitive people. . . . I know of no industrial partnership among the negroes of the North, many of whom are from stocks which have been long free. It is in just such ways that we should expect the lack of the inherited motives which are the source of power of the English race, to manifest itself in the Africans. The success of the white people has been due to the coincident development of many different capacities, any one of which failing, the race could not have attained the large measure of success which it has won.

Among these many moral features, which are spun together into the strong bonds of our society, we must count the monogamic motive. On the sacredness of the marriage relation depends the development of the stocks of families, with their inheritances of traditions from generation to generation. . . . [The] family sense remains to be developed among the negroes. In a long and intimate connection with this folk, I have never heard a [Negro] refer to his grandfather, and any reference to their parents is rare. The negro must be provided with these motives of the household; he must be made faithful to the marriage bond, and taught the sense of ancestry. This, it is plain, is a difficult task to accomplish, for the reason that the regard for the forefathers was mainly developed in a state of society through which the negro did not pass, and to which he cannot be subjected. It came from a time when, as in the feudal period, men inherited privileges as they do not in our existing commonwealth. Marital faith, however, may be inculcated by social laws, and the ancestral sense may possibly be re-enforced and extended by the diffusion of knowledge concerning the laws of heredity. . . .

Another department of education in which the negro greatly needs training is in politics. It has been a matter of surprise to many people who conceive the Africans as differing from the men of our own race in color alone, that the negroes have, in all their political action so far, disappointed what seemed to be reasonable expectations. At the time just after the war when they were in control of the States where they had just been slaves, they made a most ignominious failure in government. Since the white people regained power, they have submitted themselves in all political matters to their control. In part, this resubjugation of the blacks has doubtless been due to their fears; they are indeed an exceedingly timid people, their race education, both in the African ages and in their relatively brief American life, has altogether tended to make them fearful: in larger part it is due to the lack of those instincts of government which a peculiar series of experiences have developed in the English folk. . . .

The Education of Negroes*

HOWARD ODUM

If Negroes do have inferior brains and little intelligence, as Professor Bean and most psychologists of the day believed, these facts have important implications for education. Not only should whites and Negroes be educated separately, but they should be prepared for differing roles in society. Their education should involve different curricula and different methods of teaching. A course of study adapted to the needs and capacities of one race would ill suit those of the other. In the early 20th century, many social scientists and educators concerned themselves with these issues. Many of them were segregationists who considered themselves friends of the Negro and sincerely interested in advancing the race. To them, segregated schools were not a device for discriminating against Negroes; they were instead the only means of meeting the educational needs of two unequal races. In the following excerpt, sociologist Howard Odum comments on several aspects of Negro education from the vantage point of such a segregationist. It should be noted that Professor Odum, who later became one of the nation's most distinguished sociologists, changed his racial views drastically after he published the passages reprinted below. From his position at the University of North Carolina, he did much to awaken the South to the need for better treatment of Negroes. The views printed here, then, are not typical of Professor Odum's mature thoughts on Negro education; they are instead representative of those of many social scientists and educators in the years before World War I.

. . . The mind of the Negro is easily sensitive to sound, and words which are sounded in sequence, similar sounding words or words of alliterative sound are retained by the negro child. They are very fond

*Reprinted from Howard Odum, *Social and Mental Traits of the Negro* (New York: Columbia University Press, 1910), pp. 37-50. This work is Vol. 99 of Columbia University *Studies in History, Economics, and Public Law.*

of riddles stated in rhymes and take delight in remembering the answers to them. They learn readily to do things by imitation and become comparatively skilful in a short time. They remember names and faces well. However, there are many negro children who have an almost total lack of mental perception, whose minds are so dense that they can scarcely learn anything. The percentage of such cases increases with age.

In the school room such qualities as have been mentioned are manifested in interest and attentiveness. Negro children study diligently for short periods, and are quick to try to think. Exceptional cases of the extremes are more marked than among whites. Reading, writing and simple arithmetic are readily learned by the negroes; spelling is more difficult, perhaps because of their tendency to follow sound only. History in the simpler stories is easier for them than geography. In their language lessons they compose interesting sentences but they cannot overcome their habits and forms of speech gained at home and the inherent tendency toward mingling thoughts to a degree that outruns the ability for any continued expression of separate ideas. They have vivid but general and vague imaginations; as far as they go they form mental images quickly. The brightest students are those from nine to thirteen years of age; the clearest minds seem to be found from ten to twelve years of age. Few are found over fourteen years old who display any ability or clearness of mind on the one hand, or any brightness on the other. Experiments with negro children seem to show that the age of greatest brightness is later than that of greatest ability. By brightness is meant quickness and aptness in the doing and learning of simpler things; by ability is meant the power to grasp and hold that which confronts the mind. In both boys and girls among the negroes the highest brightness seems to be thirteen years; the highest ability for boys was found to be eight years and for the girls nine years. With white children ability increases and brightness decreases with age. As a rule, after negro children become older than ten or twelve years, their development is physical rather than mental; whatever of mental ability in the child gave promise of worth to be recognized in later years is crowded out by the coarser physical growth. In the small community few negro children over thirteen years of age attend school. It thus happens that with all the brightness and other good qualities of negro children, they attain little in the intellectual way beyond childhood. Even with better advantages offered, and under competent instruction in all cases, they would face tremendous odds. . . .

Back of the child, and affecting him both directly and indirectly, are the characteristics of the race. The Negro has little home con-science or love of home, no local attachment of the better sort. He does not know in many cases for months or years the whereabouts of his brother and sister or even parents, nor does he concern himself about their welfare. He has no pride of ancestry, and he is not in-fluenced by the lives of great men. The Negro has few ideals and perhaps no lasting adherence to an aspiration toward real worth. He has little conception of the meaning of virtue, truth, honor, man-hood, integrity. He is shiftless, untidy, and indolent; he would live "coolly in the shadow of his skin." The migratory or roving tendency seems to be a natural one to him, perhaps the outcome of an easy-going indolence seeking freedom to indulge itself and seeking to avoid all circumstances which would tend to restrict its freedom. The Negro shirks details and difficult tasks; he is incapable of turning his mind toward any other subject when once morbid curiosity holds his attention. He does not know the value of his word or the meaning of words in general. He utters phrases suited to his own fancy without regard to their meaning and forms conclusions in his mind which give him pleasure. He recognizes no causal relation between stability and prosperity, whether it be in reference to his local abode or his work. The Negro is improvident and extravagant; lazy rather than indus-trious, faithful in the performance of certain duties, without vindic-tiveness, he yet has a reasonable amount of physical endurance. But he lacks initiative; he is often dishonest and untruthful. He is over-religious and superstitious. The Negro suspects his own race and the white race as well; his mind does not conceive of faith in humanity—he does not comprehend it.

While for the most part negro children are cheerful, the older negroes are less so than formerly. Instead of the one-time good-nature, a spirit of moroseness and sullenness is developing. Negro children are easily susceptible to all influences brought to bear upon them. It has been observed that the Negro is lacking in morals, so far as personal purity and chastity are concerned. All phases of indecent subjects are discussed in the presence of children. As a matter of fact, the prevalence of habitual immorality is understood by all—the chil-dren grow up after the manner of the older ones, feeling that the situation is but a natural one. . . .

The young educated negroes are not a force for good in the com-munity but for evil. The Negro quickly outgrows the influence and control of his instructors; especially has this been noted in cases where the whites have taught them. These young negroes are not in sympathy with their parents; they appear to neglect them more than those who are not "educated." They feel that manual labor is beneath their dignity; they are fitted to do no other. They sneer at the idea of work, and they thus spread dissatisfaction among the members of their race. They imitate the whites and believe themselves thereby similar to them. They love only the show of apparent results and do not care for the details of attainment. They have not rejected vicious practices in their own lives nor condemned them in theory; on the contrary they have chosen to practice them and to condone the vices which are increasing in the race to its rapid deterioration. They uphold immorality and wish to ostracize any who assist the white man contrary to their own notions, thinking all the while that they are manifesting a spirit of race loyalty. It is clear that their moral natures are miserably perverted. Such a statement should not be interpreted as abusing the Negro; for, considering the putrid moral air he breathes and that there is no light to nourish his spiritual instincts, there could be no other outcome. Despite the excuse, however, the facts remain unchanged. The negro schools taught under present conditions have not produced the desired results; conducted according to the white man's own methods they have been unsatisfactory. . . .

It is clear that, at least for some time to come, the Negro must have [Negro] teachers in the school room. The school is the only place where a change of home life can be affected to any marked degree and where moral, physical and hygienic education can be obtained. This must necessarily take more than a generation. And it must be begun by the negroes under the supervision of the white man. It is furthermore true that the negro teacher should have means and methods for his use which are specially adapted to the proper training of his children, and he should have the careful co-operation and supervision of the whites. There are certain conditions which must be met by the negroes which do not obtain among the whites; and it is but just that when supervision, recognizing this difference, should better adapt means needed for the colored teacher's use. Here are children who must cope with tremendous odds in inherited tendencies and environment. They are different in every particular from the white children; the basis on which their education must rest is different from that of the white children. And yet under white supervision, they are given the same books, the same methods and the same grade of methods, and are required to learn as the white children do. The Negro is condemned because he thinks himself the white man's equal, and still we say to his children: You must use the same methods and the same degree of perseverance if you are to get anything out of school. It is complained that they learn too much, and it is complained that they can not learn at all and are incapable of receiving an education. In each case the Negro is compared with the whites. The logic of the situation is all wrong; the methods would appear to be wrong. In addition to the fact that the children of the two races have lived under such different educative influences and therefore need different matter and methods, the text books used in the first grade are especially suited to the whites and not suited to the negroes. To illustrate, turn through the pages of the first and second or third grade readers used by negro children in the schools. Such books are used for reader, spelling book, for writing exercises, and they often use no other text. The pages are illustrated with pictures in colors, and in every case where persons are involved they are pictures of white boys and girls with rosy cheeks and pretty features. These children have toys and pets and comforts, and all that luxury without labor could demand. The simple stories are of these boys and girls at play, of their dolls and toys and friends. The stories are varied, and are illustrated with the view to interesting children; and properly so. But what is the state of interest with which the negro child reads of things which are not his and can never be? . . .

The suggestion made here is that the text books of the first years for the negroes should be very different from those of the white children. It is hoped that the suggestion will merit serious consideration and to this end brief explanation is given. No outline of the proposed books will be given here but the general plan may be indicated. New text books are desirable for two main reasons: First, books are needed which are especially suited to the negroes as a race, to develop the negro child *within his race.* The second may be stated more fully: Text books are needed which are especially adapted to the negro *mind,* texts based on the most accurate and sympathetic knowledge of the characteristics of the Negro, which comprehend the peculiar needs of negro children, which are carefully planned and graded to teach the things fundamental in their proper education. It is essential that details be taught from the very beginning, and by constant drill the habit of doing things with accuracy be forced. The constant repetition of little things, done in order, might overcome much of the tendency in the Negro for carelessness and instability. But if any such results are to be hoped for, they must be obtained before the pupil goes beyond fourteen years of age; here the physical brain in the Negro reaches its maturity, and nearly all that can be done for a generation must be done by methods suited to the children.[1]

Let the influences upon the negro child, at least so far as the school is able to effect this end, lead him toward the unquestioning acceptance of the fact that his is a different race from the white, and properly so; that it always has been and always will be; that it is not a discredit not to be able to do as the whites, and that it is not necessarily a credit to imitate the life of the white man. Let him not measure his work by the white child's achievement. If there were no impossible fancies of being like the whites, or the constant thought of being below them, slight progress might bring the teacher and pupil to some consciousness of the degraded condition of their race. Let the negro children read stories of pioneer days, and of those who have worked their way up through the years; let such lessons be designed to teach that labor is honorable and idleness degrading. He may learn from reading stories of Africa how much better off he is than his cousins. Let him read stories of his own people, of whom there are hundreds of stories told of fidelity to duty and trust; stories of little homes with the family, and what attractions are possible for the clean negro home; of neat cottages and houses, descriptions of rooms and yards; of cleanliness and its necessity; of everyday life and what to do in the home, of fresh air and sun-light— stories of health and happiness, of labor and honor, of things interesting in the telling, but of vital import as they pertain to the everyday life of the children themselves. Then there should be many nature stories, of animals and crops, of planting and growing seed, of birds and country life. Simple rhymes and poems specially chosen for the purpose would be inserted at frequent intervals—all of which would be arranged with proper illustrations and the same pedagogical principles of teaching the reading, writing and spelling. This would have

[1]This idea was widely believed by segregationists and scientific racists. It was based on the contention that the sutures of the Negro brain knit firmly together at about the age of puberty, and thus effectively end the physical growth of Negroes. After psychologists began to measure intelligence by IQ tests, they found that the average scores of Negroes actually *declined* after about age 12 or 14. They took this as proof that the Negro brain had ceased to grow. Since the physiology of this idea is discredited, it seems likely that the decline in IQ scores (which is still often observed) is due to the compounded effects of increasingly inadequate education and environment.

its positive value and it would have its negative value. While the negro child is interested in his own matters he will not be incited to wish for the white man's conditions of life or for his nature. Until some such methods have placed the negro child on a firm basis, the Negro can never achieve permanent results in his civilization. . . .

. . . In all exercises the methods should be reasonable; the negro child needs simpler exercises than does the white child. However, each should be designed with a special purpose in view. Negroes are rarely open to reason; here they need to see things in their details rather than in the total appearance. They need to learn the real meaning of a few words rather than the sound of many. Boys and girls who are sent to the board to write sentences illustrating the meaning and use of common words like *are, the, boy, girl,* compose many sentences containing admonitions as to boys and girls stealing, telling lies, and similar sins. And yet they manifest no practical knowledge whatever of the meaning of the words; they think of the sound of the words and the entire sentence and of a pictured favorable impression made upon the teacher, or their own sense of "oughtness" and what they know to be the right sentiment. So it is with *right* and *wrong, heaven* and *hell,* and other words commonly used by negro children. Here again this method may help to resurrect the conscience of the Negro and move his intellect, and if it is possible to eradicate the criminal tendencies, it can best be begun in the school room. Special passages selected from the Bible and placed in the back of the book for morning reading or home reading might greatly assist in teaching the scriptures to the negroes, and perhaps in time, moral principles would be inculcated.

In Defense of
Southern Race Policies*

PHILIP ALEXANDER BRUCE

In the two generations after 1890, the racial views of historians were not notably different from those of southern segregationists. Historians were usually less extreme in their rhetoric, but they questioned few of the South's racial policies and fewer still of the premises upon which those policies rested. Indeed, historians made a notable contribution to the evolution of southern race policy after 1890 by placing the authority of history behind white supremacy. The following essay by the Virginia historian Philip Alexander Bruce admirably illustrates the large areas of agreement between historians and segregationists. The racial attitudes implicit in the essay were shared not only by southern segregationists and disfranchisers but by most historians who wrote on 19th-century America. Like the most outspoken segregationist, Bruce was concerned with miscegenation; and he, too, assumed that racial policy is properly controlled by whites, that the Negro's shortcomings and not white bigotry make white supremacy necessary, that "outsiders" understand neither the Negro nor southern race problems, that in the racial controversies of the 19th century the white South was universally correct, that Negroes are inferior beings.

It has been the habit, in recent years, to contrast the statesmanship of the new South unfavorably with the statesmanship of the old. This depreciatory estimate is perhaps, on the whole, not unjust if we restrict our gaze to the Southern representation in Congress under the new order, although that representation has been marked by a high degree of integrity and patriotism. But the really constructive

---

* Reprinted from Philip Alexander Bruce, "Evolution of the Negro Problem," *Sewanee Review*, Vol. XIX (October, 1911), pp. 385-99.

statesmen of the South since the war have not been found in Washington. They must be looked for in the seats of the State assemblies and city councils, on the benches of the higher courts, and in the chairs of the colleges. The ablest Southerners have been so much occupied with legislating in local matters that they have had little time or inclination to interest themselves in national matters. The rising towns and cities, the smoke of innumerable factories, the thick network of railways, the scientific and varied agriculture, the advanced colleges, and the expanding system of public schools,—these are the solid and permanent monuments of the post-bellum statesmanship of the South,—not international treaties, as of old, or vast additions to the public domain, or presidents in the White House, or brilliant orators in the Senate. And they are the monuments, not really because of what they are in themselves, but rather because they have been rendered possible by the wisdom and firmness of the local legislators of the Southern States in fixing the relations of the two races upon the precise footing which the wellbeing of that section in all its aspects, moral and social, economic and political, called for. Never in the previous history of those States, whether in its local or national bearing, had a problem of so complex a nature and so momentous an import, been presented to the consideration of her public men; and if in the treatment of that problem they have not won the general reputation for constructive ability which their fathers won under the former system, it is because their efforts have been diffused over a wide and obscure local area, instead of being concentrated in the halls of Congress at Washington.

The most notable achievements of this constructive local statesmanship consist of five great enactments, namely, the practical disfranchisement of the negro, the prohibition of the intermarriage of the races, the interdiction of their co-education, their separation in all public conveyances, and their domiciliary segregation in the cities.

First in importance, because looked upon as absolutely necessary to the preservation of Southern society, was the law which deprived the mass of the negroes of the right to vote. This law belongs to a category of its own. It has no direct connection with the four other enactments I have mentioned, even to the extent of aiming to prevent the blacks from acquiring social equality with the whites, which would follow ultimately,—certainly in a measurable degree,—should the intermarriage of the races, their co-education, and indiscriminate commingling in public conveyances and in residential sections of cities, be permitted. Nor does it seek, like the four other enactments, to promote the peaceful relations of the two races by diminishing the number of points of contact which are likely to cause friction. It is true that the practical disfranchisement of the negro has fostered goodwill between the two, but it has done so by reducing the amount of injury which he could inflict on the interests of the white people.

In passing the act of disfranchisement, the South intended deliberately to repossess herself of a right which the North, in the hour of passion, had taken from her; namely, the right to fix the political status of the freedman. She quietly drew a sponge over all the alien legislation defining that status, leaving it precisely where it was before the Republican majority in Congress had had time to interpose. In one sense, the act of disfranchisement was a step backward; but it was a step backward with the intention of taking such a step forward ultimately as circumstances should then show to be safe. It was not a constructive act, like the other acts which I have named, but a destructive act, both in spirit and in operation, because it was essentially an act of repeal.

In rushing in and arbitrarily and prematurely requiring the South to enfranchise the indigent and illiterate black man almost as soon as he had obtained his freedom, the North dislocated hopelessly for a time that judicious evolutionary process through which negro suffrage would have passed, had the Southern people been left to confer that right gradually and to regulate its exercise. As it is, the franchise is the one question relating to the blacks, which, forty-five years after their emancipation, continues in a state of uncertainty; and this is due directly to Northern interference. The North did not dictate that negroes should be permitted to marry with the whites; or that black children should be educated with whites in the public schools; or that white people and black people should be required to ride in the same railway coaches, or to live together in the same city blocks. Had Congress attempted to interpose in the settlement of these questions, there would have been the same check in their orderly evolution as there was in the orderly evolution of the suffrage. Confusion would have at once resulted; and those branches of the negro problem would have remained unsolved, to the serious embroilment of the two races.

The four other measures which I have enumerated stand upon a footing different from that of the act of disfranchisement. They represent four consecutive stages in the evolution of the negro problem, and reflect the harmonious and consistent progress which that problem has made toward a permanent settlement. These enactments could not all have been adopted together in the beginning without inflicting a hardship, or at least without causing grave inconvenience, simply because the conditions then prevailing were not ripe for the passage of all four at once. For two alone were those conditions really ripe; namely, the prohibition of intermarriage, and the interdiction of co-education.

It was natural from a social point of view, and wise from a political, that the white people, from the inauguration of the new order, should have been solicitous that the intermarriage of whites and blacks should not be sanctioned by law. The instinct of race preservation even more than opposition to social equality, dictated this attitude. It is true that, during the existence of the institution of slavery, illicit cohabitation had taken place to such an extent that mulattoes made up an important section of the population of each Southern community. But these mulattoes took the status of the black parent, not of the white, even though the mother was of the latter blood. Had marriage between the two races been suffered after the war, the offspring of these unions would have, legally and morally, been entitled to the status of the white parent; and as the number of such unions increased, such offspring would, in time, have actually acquired that status. As education developed in them a greater ability to accumulate wealth, mongrelization would have steadily advanced in social respectability, until it is presumable that there would have arisen a large number of legitimate mulattoes who, through their white parents, had obtained an unquestionable social position. With intermarriage made valid, the tendency of every community in which negroes predominated numerically would have been towards Africanization; for, first, the existence of the right of intermarriage would have encouraged illicit as well as legitimate sexual commerce between the races by promoting social equality; and secondly, in that considerable section of the white population which would have declined to affiliate with the blacks it would have created a disposition to emigrate. As the intermixture progressed, the white persons who would have been revolted by the spectacle of the legal miscegenation which was going on, would have been gradually driven out by the force of their intense repugnance to the prevailing conditions, until there would have been left a residuum of white families unopposed to the commingling of their own blood with the blood of the negro.

But the force of the law which prohibits the intermarriage of whites and blacks is most fully seen in the effect which it has had in diminishing illicit sexual intercourse between them by discouraging their social equality. During the existence of slavery, the mulattoes formed a proportion of the negro population which, numerically, steadily maintained itself even if it did not actually increase. As long as the negress was a slave, there was no danger of her presuming upon an immoral intimacy,—a fact well known to her white paramour for his encouragement,—and her subservience necessarily made her more open to advances. Since the revolution in the relations of the two races which was brought about by emancipation, the number of mulattoes has, to the body of the population, relatively if not absolutely declined. It is only in the Southern cities that they are to-day really noticeable even in the African quarters; and not even there to the extent observable twenty or thirty years ago. One may visit the public schools for the negroes in the cities without seeing perhaps half a dozen children in each room whose complexions reveal a white parentage on one side. The proportion of those whose darkness of skin indicates a black parentage on both sides for at least one generation and a half, is, in comparison, overwhelming. The indiscriminate intermarriage of blacks and mulattoes since the war has been steadily reducing the number of mulattoes whose first infusion of white blood was obtained during the period of slavery, while the reserve of the white men of the new generation has prevented the replacement ... of the number thus lost. That there is still a considerable proportion of mulattoes in the cities is to be largely attributed to the facilities there for a casual and passing illicit sexual commerce unattended by any danger of exposure for the white participant, or risk of being held legally responsible for the offspring resulting. It is also, in some degree, attributable to the influx of foreigners in recent years, men not likely to be led by prejudice or fear of notoriety to shrink from even permanent illegitimate relations with negresses. In the rural districts of the South, the number of mulattoes is now so small as to attract no notice whatever. The explanation is obvious,—apart from the general influences which are steadily separating the races, the white man in the country is held back by the certainty that an intrigue will sooner or later become known, or by apprehension lest he may, at any time, be compelled to assume some responsibility for the fruit of the illicit cohabitation.

In either event, his standing in his own community would suffer lasting injury.

The immediate effect of the decline in the illicit sexual intercourse between the two races[1] is to promote a steady reversion in the negroes to the original pure African type, a fact that, in the next few generations, will be perceptible in their general moral and intellectual character. The leading men of the race so far have been of mixed blood.[2] It remains to be seen whether this pure African type can produce an equal number of persons of considerable intellectual capacity. With a complete reversion to the original type, the last ground for anticipating even partial amalgamation of the two races will pass away. The first great law touching the freedman adopted by the South has already fully accomplished its purpose; the integrity of the white race has been preserved not only from destruction but even from partial deterioration. Intermarriage is now an impossible factor as affecting that integrity, and illicit sexual commerce a negligible one.

The second constructive law adopted by the South in the regular evolution of the negro problem forbade the co-education of the two races in the public schools. As with the evils of miscegenation, so with the evils of co-education—they were foreseen by the Southern people so soon as legislation began to be enacted to define the status of the freedman. A feeling of repulsion was reflected in both measures,—

---

[1]There is little concrete evidence to support any facet of Bruce's discussion of racial intermixture. There is no evidence to indicate that the amount of illicit racial intercourse declined appreciably after emancipation, or that Negroes were reverting "to the original pure African type." In fact, the dependent status of Negroes under segregation left Negro women at the mercy of white men as had been the case during slavery. Geneticist Curt Stern estimated in 1954 that "about two thirds of the genetic building material of the United States Negro comes from Africa and about one third from Europe." See Curt Stern, "The Biology of the Negro," *Scientific American*, Vol. CXCI (October, 1954), pp. 81-85.

[2]Historian Richard Bardolph, who has made the most detailed study of distinguished Negro leaders, has written as follows: "Most distinguished Negroes have been persons of mixed blood, a phenomenon now ascribed by scholars not to inherent white superiority but to the huge differential in the cultural heritage of the two races; the fact that the mothers of mixed Negroes have been the choicest colored specimens that the white man could commandeer; the reinforcement of this biological selection by a tendency for mulattoes to draw away from blacks by marrying their own kind, and for the most successful blacks to marry into the lighter-skinned group, so that Negro talent became increasingly concentrated there. More important still, the Negro of lighter skin, in slavery and freedom, was afforded far greater indulgence by the white man; and the Negro himself, urged by social environment, tended to defer to his half-white cousin." Richard Bardolph, *The Negro Vanguard* (New York: Random House, Inc., 1959), p. 16. Whether this phenomenon is as true today as it once was seems highly problematical.

a repulsion aroused primarily by the instinct of race preservation; only in the case of intermarriage, it was chiefly physical; in the case of co-education mainly ethical. The principal reason for the repugnance which the Southern whites exhibited from the start to the promiscuous commingling of white and black children in the same school-room was not only that it would quickly break down the social barriers that kept the two races apart, but would certainly expose the white children, especially the girls, to polluting and debasing influences. The free and easy associations of a public school would be very different in their impression on character from the guarded association of the plantation in the time of slavery. Kind as was the feeling of most masters and mistresses for their bondsmen, they nevertheless had an ineradicable and unalterable conviction as to certain characteristics of the race as a whole,—the indifference to chastity in the females, the lewdness of the males, the physical uncleanliness, the unrefined manners, and the generally careless habits of life distinguishing so many of both sexes alike. The class of whites who had never owned a slave were as resolutely hostile to co-education as the class above them who had owned many slaves; but they were more influenced by fear of social equality than by apprehension of moral contamination, though this too, in their case, was also present, but perhaps not to the same degree. Naturally, this opposition to co-education was particularly strong in all classes of white citizens immediately after the negro acquired his freedom, for then they had been in the habit of looking on him only as a slave who possessed no social position whatever in the community to which he belonged. So fully was this opposition known even to the "carpetbag" governments, that only in South Carolina and Texas was provision made for mixed schools,—a provision soon repealed in Texas, while in South Carolina it remained entirely unenforceable. Had such a law been adopted throughout the Southern States, it would have simply meant that the whites would, as a body, have declined to send their children to the public school.

The third great constructive law in the practical evolution of the negro problem was not passed by the Southern people to preserve their blood integrity, like the law prohibiting intermarriage; nor to conserve their purity of morals and manners, like the law forbidding co-education; nor like both these laws, to discourage social equality. The primary object of the statute requiring the separation of the races in public vehicles of conveyance was simply to promote the personal comfort and safety of the whites. It was offensive to them to be brought in such close physical contact with the new negro; and in addition, they were anxious to diminish the chances of personal conflict so likely to arise at any moment when whites and blacks who are strangers to each other, assemble under the same roof. Had any question of the preservation of the whites' integrity of blood or morality been involved in the association of the races in public conveyances, their separation there would have been required as soon after emancipation as the prohibition of their intermarriage or co-education, although at that time, owing to the poverty of the Southern railways, an almost intolerable burden would have been imposed upon the resources of these lines of transporation. As the white and black populations expanded, and at the same time became more alienated from each other with the passing of the older generation, and as the regular volume of travel increased, the physical repulsiveness of indiscriminate race mixture in public conveyances grew more acute, and the danger of personal conflicts also augmented. The railways, in the meanwhile, had been steadily advancing in prosperity, and were now in a position to supply the double accommodations that would be called for by the separation of the races. The white people, perceiving this fact, demanded the change, and the railways offered no serious opposition. A more useful law was never inserted in the Southern statute book. No one who remembers the former promiscuous commingling of whites and blacks in the Southern trains can fail to recall the scenes of violence witnessed there in consequence of the aggressive attitude of negroes inflamed by drink.[3] Such scenes between the races are no longer possible; and that fact alone has done much to promote a more friendly relation between them in all the walks of life in which they still meet.

The fourth great constructive enactment came, not in the form of a state statute, but of a municipal ordinance, which has already been adopted by the governing bodies of nearly all the large cities of the

---

[3]Here is an example of the segregationists' practice of judging Negroes solely by their race. Bruce's complaints about drunk Negroes led him to insist upon segregating Negroes rather than drunks. Note that drunkenness among Negroes becomes an argument for segregating Negroes, but drunkenness among whites leads to no similar demand for segregation. It seems logical to say that race rather than intoxication was Bruce's real concern. Bruce's reference to the likelihood of interracial violence on integrated public conveyances is another instance of the inconsistency of segregationists. Earlier he spoke of the instinct of race preservation which had led whites to pass laws prohibiting intermarriage. One would think that if "race preservation" were instinctive such laws would be unnecessary. Now we are told that interracial contact will produce not intermarriage but violence.

South; and, in a few more years, is quite certain to be adopted by the remainder. This additional enactment requires the domiciliary segregation of the races. Like the three great constructive laws which preceded it, it is a measure that looks to the preservation of something that the whites regard as essential to their welfare. First, as we have seen, they passed an act to preserve their race integrity; secondly, an act to preserve their integrity of morals and manners; thirdly, an act to preserve their comfort, convenience, and safety in travelling. Now a fourth act is passed, to preserve the value of property which has been seriously threatened with deterioration by the encroachment of the urban black population on districts hitherto entirely occupied by whites. This new measure is an indication, not so much of the accumulation of holdings by the negroes (although it does mean this too to a certain extent), as of their numerical increase in the towns; largely by immigration from the country. It is the black tenant rather than the black purchaser, whose intrusion, in most cases involuntary, has alarmed so many white owners of property. The bulk of these black tenants are unable to pay the rents which the previous white tenants had been paying; and this fact, coupled with the mere presence of negroes on the ground, has led to the decline in the value of all tenements from which they have practically ousted the white occupants.

A Historian's View*
of the Negro

HUBERT HOWE BANCROFT

Segregationist thought rests ultimately upon contempt for Negroes as human beings. This contempt is most obvious among extremists, though it has often appeared in the writings of scholars. The following excerpt from the memoirs of the distinguished historian Hubert Howe Bancroft illustrates the extent to which historians sometimes shared the blatant racism of extremists. Bancroft was a New Englander of abolitionist background, and his espousal of such extreme views is another measure of the difficulties faced by Negroes in the two generations after 1890. The race had to overcome the racism not only of poor whites and political demagogues, but of more "responsible" men as well. This is a major reason for the Negroes' inability to protect themselves even in minimum ways: virtually all elements of American society supported (or at least acquiesced in) segregation, disfranchisement, and discrimination. Historians who shared Bancroft's views, even when expressed less caustically, could hardly view American history and the Negro's role therein with an open mind.

Turning to the African in our midst we find conditions never elsewhere existing in the history of humanity.

The Anglo-African [i.e., the American Negro] presents a pathetic picture, a picture more touching than that of Russian Jew or Armenian Christian. However white within he must forever appear in black without. However learned he may become, however lofty his ideals or high his aspirations he must wear the badge of ignorance and servitude, he and his children forever. God hath made him so; man has

---

*Reprinted from Hubert Howe Bancroft, *Retrospection* (New York: Bancroft Co., 1912), pp. 367-74.

re-stamped him; time brings no relief. It was a cruel kindness to enslave him; it was cruelty pure and simple to enfranchise him.

Sentimentalists say that our forefathers did the African a wrong when they enslaved him, and that we owe him reparation. It does not so appear to me. Slaves were obtained from different tribes constantly at war with each other, as Mandinga, Congo, Senegal, and Nard, each speaking a language which the other did not understand.

The slaver found the object of his pursuit, as a rule, an enslaved cannibal in the hands of cannibals, to be sold or else to be killed and eaten. On the horrible slave-ships his condition was but little improved. It was from such atrocities as these that the southern planter rescued him, gave him work and made him happy. True, he did not buy him from benevolence but for profit. It was not the purpose of the slave-trade, the most infamous of human deeds since the coming of Christ, to make the negro happy. Further, only a few thousand were rescued from cannibalism, whereas millions became slaves.

It is right and proper that we should do what we can for the amelioration of the condition of that unfortunate people, but not on the ground of the cruelties or injustice practised by others.

For if ever we owed the negro aught we paid the debt many times in the [civil] war which though not for him was because of him.

When all is said, the fact remains that had the early slave-traders read and followed the American declaration of human rights, so emphasized by human wrongs, the progenitors of our Africans would have been killed and eaten, and these United States thereby have been saved much trouble, past and future. But fate willed it otherwise, and the end is not yet. . . .

It was right for us to set the negro free. It was our necessity, not his. We have passed the period when we can hold our fellow-man in slavery and live. But we bungled more in liberating than in enslaving him. . . .

Were it not better frankly to admit that the freed African in America is a failure, and that when made free he should have been sent away?

He is a failure here, for effective work is not to be obtained from him except under compulsion. As an American citizen he is a monstrosity.

If we could utilize our African citizens in factories and on farms it would be an advantage to all concerned, but the negro is good for nothing as a working-man, or for anything else, except on the southern plantations, and he is not all that he might be there.

The African is lazy and licentious. It is not altogether the fault of the white man that he is so, nor yet altogether his own fault. It is kismet. The animal in him overbalances the mental. He will work only as necessity requires. At least three millions out of the ever-increasing ten millions encamped upon us live without work. The black man is trifling; he lacks application; he has neither continuous purpose nor continuous effort; he is satisfied simply to live and enjoy. And why not? Wall street might profit by his philosophy.

We are told by good people of the sentimental school, as before remarked, that we have wronged the African, that notwithstanding the clothes and colored schools we have given him, the lessons in grace and refinement, and the several other gifts of the intellectual life, to say nothing of the bestowal of equal rights and American citizenship, that we are still in his debt.

This is discouraging.

To our fair land of America he was brought a captive—a happy captive one would think—and in a genial clime was given work, not too severe, as the change from meat diet to corn must be considered, and though for wholesome discipline cut with the whip a little sometimes when he moved too slowly.

And on his part, did he pine away and grow pale under his inhuman wrong? Ah, no! He laughed and grew fat, threw care to the winds, and slept undisturbed by thoughts of having to go into the boiling pot for somebody's breakfast in the morning. Thus on these southern plantations for a century or more he was made the happiest of mortals, as indeed from first to last he was the most fortunate. His troubles came with emancipation; more came with enfranchisement; but he had to be emancipated; it was necessity; civilization must be allowed to move on unobstructed.

We did more than that. We gave him religion, which he took to greedily. We gave him his freedom, but he did not know what to do with it, and he gained from it no new happiness. We gave him American citizenship, the cheapest thing we had. . . . And with the franchise in his pocket, price of votes from fifty cents to two dollars, he was left to propagate piccaninnies and idle life away in peace and happiness.

However horrid the crime of human slavery, however repulsive in all its forms and unprofitable in its operations, the fact remains that the negro was never so well off, so happy and contented as when he was the chattel of the chivalrous south. It was as if God's curse of Canaan was but a covert benediction, for until he found the blessings of bondage in North America his lot was truly a piteous one, a savage, and the master or the slave of savages.

A million of the finest young men the sun ever shone upon, slaughtered [in the Civil War] because of these Africans, and some billions of money and property sacrificed—all together more than the whole continent of Africa and all its people are worth. I should call the debt paid, if indeed it ever existed. . . .

In all this I mean no unkindness to the negro, and offer no excuse for his enslavement. I have never forgotten his wrongs as they were told to me at my mother's knee. I have never wavered in my loyalty to him since as a small boy I used to drive wagon loads of him on his way to freedom hidden under the straw, but I cannot change from hot to cold and back again so often or so quickly as some of my super-sensitive friends. . . .

One of the most intricate problems of population before the American people, and one likely to be with us, is that of the African. The subject varies with the varying mood of the American mind, sentimentalism having entered into it largely of late. Every one knows that as an economic asset the freed slave diminished in value, while in the end the employer gained, as free labor is cheaper than slave labor.

The relative influence for good or evil of the African, the Asiatic, and the European in our midst lies chiefly in the difference between adoption and absorption. If we could disabuse our minds of the sentiment that it is necessary forever to debase American blood and institutions by the infusion of low alien elements, whether in colors black, white, or yellow, receive and hold foreigners as foreigners for whatsoever they prove themselves to be worth, not necessarily to be admitted into our political household as members with all rights and privileges; assigning them their proper place, treating them fairly, without being forced to divide and re-divide with them our patrimony, we might better be able to preserve our own integrity while giving higher service to them.

 . . . How fast and how far in one brief century have we drifted from the plans and purposes of the founders of this republic! We have made ten millions of negroes, of a servile race and antecedents,

whose fathers were slaves and themselves in intellect, in natural pro-
clivities, not too far removed from the jungles of Africa, our equals,
politically and some would have it so socially were it possible—a blot
upon our name and nation, and now we know not what to do with
them. We cannot kill them, or lose them, and they will not be driven
by any force at our present command to herd themselves on some
distant island or continent.

Further, we do not need the negro for any purpose, and never
shall. We did not need the Indian and so eliminated him. We cannot
so dispose of the negro. He is too incompetent and unreliable for any
use; as a citizen of the commonwealth he is an unmitigated nuisance,
and judging from the past he will so remain. The ultra susceptible,
who alternately scourge and weep will say otherwise, but the facts
stand plainly out that he who runs may read if he chooses. . . .

As a laborer, bond or free, the negro is of economic value only in
certain localities and under certain conditions. The labor must be
agricultural and upon a large scale, so that he can be worked in gangs
under the eye of an overseer. Then he needs to live in a warm climate.
The cotton and tobacco fields of the south alone meet his requirements. In plantation life alone he finds happiness. To live together
under compulsion on some allotted territory would not suit the
Americanized negro. He depends upon the white man to do his
mental work, his thinking and managing for him, preferring himself
only to serve. He is by nature and habit a servant, not alone because
of his long period of enslavement, but because of his mental inferiority.

There are those who claim for the African race an intellectual
quality with Europeans, but they make out a poor case of it. Even to
Asiatics the Africans are inferior in every respect, else why when
every opportunity and encouragement was given them did they remain stationary, when Japan surged forward to the front the moment
her reluctant doors were forced open by western civilization?

Negroes and the South in Reconstruction*

CLAUDE BOWERS

Nowhere was the racism of historians more evident than in their writings on Reconstruction, and no account of Reconstruction better illustrates this than Claude Bowers' widely read The Tragic Era *(1929). In the following brief excerpt, Bowers discusses the immediate reaction of Negroes to freedom, the activities of "outsiders" among the freedmen, and the nature and purpose of the Ku Klux Klan. Especially noteworthy are Bowers' tendency toward melodrama, even luridness; his disposition to blame racial antipathy upon the gullibility of Negroes and the agitation of Radicals, carpetbaggers, and scalawags; and his willingness to condone extreme measures to preserve white supremacy. Bowers' assumption of racial inequality and Negro inferiority is evident throughout the passage reprinted below. Indeed, these passages are meaningless without that assumption.*

[Would the freedmen] harken to the advice of their former masters and mistresses? Had not their new friends from the North been at pains to teach them these were enemies? Freedom—it meant idleness, and gathering in noisy groups in the streets. Soon they were living like rats in ruined houses, in miserable shacks under bridges built with refuse lumber, in the shelter of ravines and in caves in the banks of rivers. Freedom meant throwing aside all marital obligations,[1] deserting wives and taking new ones, and in an indulgence in

---

*Reprinted from Claude Bowers, *The Tragic Era* (New York: Houghton Mifflin Co., 1929), pp. 49-53, 60-61, 198-201, 307-10.

[1] Bowers' readiness to condemn the freedmen for their immorality was typical of segregationists. Of course, Negro marriages during slavery had no legal status at all; thus most freedmen were not legally married. Bowers never felt it necessary to denounce the absence of "all marital obligations" among slaves, or the "indulgence in sexual promiscuity" which slavery encouraged among slaves. This is another example of the segregationists' double standard: one standard for things southern whites approved, another for things they disapproved. As a matter of fact, this entire excerpt is evidence of the double standard at work. Virtually every action Bowers denounced Negroes for, he condoned in whites.

sexual promiscuity that soon took its toll in the victims of consumption and venereal disease. Jubilant, and happy, the negro who had his dog and a gun for hunting, a few rags to cover his nakedness, and a dilapidated hovel in which to sleep, was in no mood to discuss work.

All over the South that summer the negroes held their jubilee. A weird wave of religious fervor swept them into a crazy frenzy, and day after day they gathered in groves where imported preachers worked on their emotions. Shouting, praying, howling, they turned their backs on the old plantation preachers, who disapproved of the methods of the visiting evangelists, who in many instances turned out to be unscrupulous organizers for the Northern Radicals. At the night the vicinity of the revivals was pillaged of poultry and vegetables on the theory that the Lord should provide. . . .

If the negroes caused some uneasiness, many of the army of occupation were more disturbing. . . . The meanest offenses of soldiers were committed against the blacks who gathered about them in childish faith, to be worse maltreated than by former masters, who, in numerous instances, interfered to protect them from the cruelty of their "deliverers." Even more cruel was the persistent effort of soldiers to instill into the negro's mind a hatred of the men with whom he would have to live after the army should march away. . . . Emissaries of radicalism were constantly inflaming the freedmen with a false sense of their importance, turning them against the native whites, encouraging their indolence with wild tales of the inevitable division of the plantation lands among them. Young colored women, gayly making their way to camps to "enjoy mah freedom," were frequently used for immoral purposes. . . .

It only remained for the Federal Government to drive the disarmed [Southern white] people to the verge of a new rebellion by stationing negro troops in the midst of their homes. Nothing short of stupendous ignorance, or brutal malignity, can explain the arming and uniforming of former slaves and setting them as guardians over the white men and their families. . . . In streets and highways [there was] . . . the spectacle of thousands of blacks with muskets and shimmering bayonets swaggering in jeering fashion before their former masters and mistresses. These colored soldiers were not so culpable as the whites who used them to torture a fallen enemy. These were children, acting as children would under the circumstances. Marching four abreast in the streets, they jostled the whites from the pavements. In rough and sullen tones the sentries challenged old crippled and emaciated men in tattered gray. So insolent did their conduct become in some communities that women no longer dared venture from their doors, and citizens in the country no longer felt it safe to go to town. Noisy—often, when intoxicated, dangerous— they gave the freedmen refusing to work a sense of racial grandeur, and encouraged the dream of the distribution of the white man's land. . . .

Meanwhile the Southern people [i.e., the whites] were fighting for the preservation of their civilization. The negroes would not work, the plantations could not produce. The freedmen clung to the illusion planted in their minds by demagogues that the economic status of the races was to be reversed through the distribution of the land among them. This cruelly false hope was being fed by private soldiers, [Freedmen's] Bureau agents, and low Northern whites circulating among the negroes on terms of social equality in the cultivation of their prospective votes.[2] "Nothing but want will bring them to their senses," wrote one Carolinian to another. At the time, however, the negroes were warding off want by prowling the highways and byways in the night for purposes of pillage. In one week, in one town in Georgia, one hundred and fifty were arrested for theft. . . .

This, then, was the combination against the peace of a fallen people—the soldiers inciting the blacks against their former masters, the Bureau agents preaching political and social equality, the white scum of the North fraternizing with the blacks in their shacks, and the thieves of the Treasury stealing cotton under the protection of Federal bayonets. And in the North, demagogic politicians and fanatics were demanding immediate negro suffrage and clamoring for the blood of Southern leaders. Why was not Jeff Davis hanged; and why was not Lee shot? . . .

Left to themselves, the negroes would have turned for leadership to the native whites, who understood them best. This was the danger. Imperative, then, that they should be taught to hate—and teachers of hate were plentiful.[3] Many of these were found among the agents of

---

[2]This passage (and others too) illustrates Bowers' contempt for whites who practiced social equality with Negroes. Like segregationists in general, Bowers refused to believe that any sane and respectable white man would practice social equality; he was forced to conclude that those who did were either degenerates or had ulterior political motives.

[3]Here is a classic example of the segregationist mind at work. As ensuing passages indicate, Bowers equated "hate" with doctrines of political, economic, and social equality. To preach "hate" to Negroes was thus to treat them as equals, tell them of their rights as American citizens, and help them achieve those rights.

the Freedmen's Bureau, and these, paid by the Government, were devoting themselves assiduously to party organization on Government time. Over the plantations these agents wandered, seeking the negroes in their cabins, and halting them at their labors in the fields, and the simple-minded freedmen were easy victims of their guile. . . .

Orators were needed as well as organizers, for open agitation was as essential as quiet management, and soon the lowest types of the abandoned whites were being sent into the South to arouse the passions of the negroes with incendiary speeches. The Bureau agents summoned them to meetings in the fields at night. "My friends," the orator would say, "you'll have your rights, won't you?" "Yes!" shouted the eager freedmen. "Shall I go back to Massachusetts and tell your brothers there that you are going to ride in the street cars with white ladies if you please?" "Yes!" came the thundering response. "That if you pay your money to go to the theater, you will sit where you please, in the best boxes if you like?" And the negroes would clap their hands and shout an affirmative reply. In North Carolina, Holden, the former Governor, was exciting their cupidity with false hopes. The year before, the State had raised one hundred thousand bales of cotton. "Whose labor made this cotton? Who got the money?"

More vicious, however, were the imported agitators "of the lowest character, destitute of principles," such as "Colonel" James Sinclair, the "fighting parson," a Uriah Heep of humility, mingling socially with the negroes, and promising them the division of the white man's acres among the blacks if they would vote the Republican ticket. One night he urged the negroes to hate their former masters and treat them with insolence and contempt, and under the exhilaration of his harangue, a negro speaker said that within ten years the problem would be what the blacks would do with the Southern whites. "If my colored brother and myself touch elbows at the polls," cried a carpetbagger in Louisiana, "why should not his child and mine stand side by side in the public schools?" . . .

Soon the imitative negroes rivaled the instructors from the North in abuse and in exaggerated demands, and one of them, speaking for the Union League at Chattanooga, advised his race to "know the true thing in politics" from "such men as Brownlow" and to "teach your children . . . that they may grow up big-mouthed Radicals." . . . And now that the revolution had come, the passions, cupidity, hates of the negroes were being aroused and constantly fed. Everywhere a new spirit of arrogance had been awakened. When an old plantation preacher told his race that the former masters were the blacks' best friends, a Radical paper noted that "there was no little muttering in the crowd." Soon the whites, especially on remote plantations, were gravely apprehensive, and an English woman living in Georgia could see nothing but tragedy ahead with the governing forces "exciting the negroes to every kind of insolent lawlessness." Then it was that the rioting began. At Norfolk, when the negroes marched belligerently through the streets rattling firearms, the races clashed, with two fatalities on each side. In Richmond, the blacks, determined to ride with the whites, rushed the street cars, and troops were necessary to restore order. In New Orleans, where separate cars were provided, the negroes demanded the right to use the cars of the whites, who appealed to General Sheridan, without avail, and the blacks triumphed, and immediately demanded mixed schools and a division of the offices. . . .

[In its early history the Ku Klux Klan confined itself to intimidating Negroes.] From the intimidation of the negroes it was an easy step to the challenging of the carpetbaggers and agitators who were lustily instilling into the black men's minds a hatred and distrust of the native whites. Thus, more than once, when the simple blacks were gathered in groups about an agitator of the lowest type, the Klansmen, lighted by torches, would appear, silently to circle the crowd until the black men fled in terror.[4] . . .

Thus the society, formed for amusement, and found effective in controlling the negroes, soon developed into an agency to combat the Loyal Leagues formed under the inspiration of the Union League Clubs of the Northern cities.

The original intent was to act for regulation and not for punishment, and there was desperate need for regulation. The crusade of hate and social equality, and more, was playing havoc with a race naturally kindly and trustful. Throughout the war, when men were far away on the battlefields, and the women were alone on far plantations with the slaves, hardly a woman was attacked. Then came the scum of Northern society, emissaries of the politicians, soldiers of fortune, and not a few degenerates, inflaming the negroes' egotism, and soon the lustful assaults began. Rape is the foul daughter of Reconstruction. . . . All over the South, white women armed

---

[4]Note the difference in Bowers' reaction to the "terror" whites caused among Negroes, and his reaction to terror Negroes caused among whites.

themselves in self-defense.[5] Before the Klan appeared, and after the Loyal Leagues had spread their poison, no respectable white woman dared venture out in the black belt unprotected. "We are in the hands of camp followers, horse-holders, cooks and bottle-washers and thieves," testified a reputable citizen of Alabama. The spectacle of negro police leading white girls to jail was not unusual in Montgomery. Among the poor, the white women of the farms taking their produce to the markets traveled in large companies as a protection against rape. In places the military and the Freedmen's Bureau offered no relief. Negroes who had criminally attacked white women, tried and sent to the penitentiary, were turned loose after a few days' incarceration. It was not until the original Klan began to ride that white women felt some sense of security.

Controlled in the beginning by men of character and substance, the plan [of Klan leaders] was to manage the freedmen by playing on their fears and superstitions. Novel schemes were often tried. Thus a night traveler, provided with a rubber sack, would stop at a negro's hut and ask for water. After "drinking" three bucketfuls, to the consternation of the trembling black, the traveler would observe that he had traveled a thousand miles in twenty-four hours and "that was the best water I have had since I was killed at the battle of Shiloh." . . .

The negroes, clustered together in their cabins, recounted these awful stories and for a time grew humble, industrious, law-abiding. . . .

In the pioneer West, vigilance committees were formed for the protection of horses and cattle; in the South, the Klan was organized for the protection of women, property, civilization itself.

With the success of the Klan in Tennessee, the organization of the society spread rapidly over the South. In the spring of 1867, when Nashville was teeming with soldiers and officers, the first national gathering of the Klan was held in the Maxwell House without being suspected. General [Nathan Bedford] Forrest had been placed at the head, with the sanction of Lee, who strongly urged that the organization be kept a purely "protective organization." This famous soldier, "The Wizard of the Saddle," had more than a touch of military genius, and he was a stern disciplinarian and, morally, a superior man. He neither drank nor swore, and he had been known to dismiss an

---

[5]Again, compare Bowers' reaction to the danger, largely imaginary, experienced by white women, and his complete lack of concern for the very real danger faced by Negro women, both before and after emancipation.

officer under his command for immorality.[6] In the midst of war, his tent, on Sundays, was converted into a church, and he had his chaplain pray before a battle. A brilliant tactician, he brought his genius to bear in the organization of the Klan forces. No one knew better how, through elusive tactics, by marching and countermarching, to deceive the eye as to the number of men in the saddle with features concealed. His predominating trait was his reverence for women.[7]

In the early phase [of the Klan] only men of the highest order were in control. . . . . Everywhere men of high order, none of whom would have countenanced crime.

---

[6]Bowers fails to state that Forrest was now head of an organization committed to extreme measures to preach white supremacy and deprive Negroes of the rights guaranteed them in Reconstruction legislation. It is a strange morality that requires of a man that he neither drink nor swear but permits him to terrorize and intimidate his fellowmen.

[7]Since Forrest had been a slave trader, it seems fair to assume that Bowers here refers only to white women.

A Politician's Defense of Segregation*

FRANK CLARK

Politicians have always been the most vociferous and eager champions of southern race policies. The new policies inaugurated between 1890 and 1910 did not have the anticipated results. The race issue, far from having been settled by segregation and disfranchisement came to pervade southern politics, demanding orthodoxy from politician and citizen alike, and encouraging extremism in both. Too often victory went to emotional demagogues whose only achievement was "out-niggering" opponents. The level of southern politics and government degenerated. Politics became a means of diverting attention from real economic and social problems, government a device for furthering the ambitions of demagogues. The following speech by Democratic Congressman Frank Clark of Florida illustrates these facts about southern politics. It is a politician's defense of racial segregation at the time segregation was being legalized and formalized, and is typical of much of what southern politicians wrote and said on this subject. For example, it illustrates the manner in which politicians used the ideas of social scientists and historians. The speech was made in support of an amendment to a pending bill, offered by Representative J. Thomas Heflin of Alabama, to segregate streetcars in Washington, D.C.

. . . On last Sunday afternoon an old negro man living in this city came to my office and spent the afternoon with my wife and myself, and I have not spent a more pleasant afternoon for years. [Applause] He belonged to my father, and he was the first human being that ever

*Reprinted from U.S. *Congressional Record,* Vol. XLII, Part 8, 60th Cong., 1st sess. (Washington, D.C.: U.S. Government Printing Office, February 22, 1908), (Appendix), pp. 38-40.

carried me out in the yard after my birth. [Applause on the Democratic side.] . . . I love that old negro man [applause], and . . . in a contest between him and others, in a physical contest, I would be found by his side protecting and defending him. [Renewed applause.] That is a sentiment that . . . northern Republicans do not understand and can not understand. [Applause.] But there is a vast difference . . . in that sentiment which every man upon this [Democratic] side of the House who lives south of [the Potomac] river can understand and the sentiment that his children and mine are to sit side by side in school. There is a vast difference in that sentiment and the sentiment that they should sit side by side with my children in a street car or in any other public conveyance.

This amendment offered by the gentleman from Alabama is not an attack upon the negro race; it is not unjust to them. . . .

I am going to vote for this amendment. I am going to do it because I think it is in the interest of the black man more so than it is in the interest of the white man, and I say this because, as is well known, in every conflict between the races the black man gets the worst of it. You bring them together and you are bound to have conflicts. You know it and I know it. There is no need of our undertaking to deceive ourselves on this question, nor is there need of inquiring who is to blame. I would not do them an injury. I would not do them a wrong, and I do not believe you can get one of them in my State who is acquainted with me to tell you that I would. . . . Having had the experience of a lifetime with them, I express it as my deliberate judgment that it is better to keep them separate—better for them, better for their race, better for everybody; and this system is working well in the State of Florida, in our larger cities, where we have street cars, and upon our steam railroads all over the State. There never has been any confusion or trouble on account of the separation of the races on public conveyances. Before the adoption of that system there was a great deal of trouble. I admit that at times it was caused by the white man. I am not holding him up as entirely blameless. . . . If you desire to reduce the chances of trouble to the minimum and subserve the best interests of all the people, you had better keep the races apart in all public conveyances. . . .

Mr. Chairman, the relations of the races in the South is the one question, I believe, above all others that has been more discussed by more people who absolutely knew nothing of it than any other question that has ever challenged American thought since the formation of this Republic. The ignorance of real conditions permeating the effusions of the theoretical defenders of the negro race would be ludicrous in the extreme if it were not for the fact that every speech, magazine article, or other publication of this character makes more difficult the proper and just settlement of one of the greatest problems that ever confronted any people. In the beginning of my remarks upon the pending amendment . . . I said that I regretted the turn which the discussion had taken. Partisanship has no place in the consideration of a question of this character. I regret that our Republican friends have seen fit to inject into the debate wholesale charges of oppression of the negro in the various Southern States, and, as is usual when such charges are made, have utterly failed to submit any proof supporting the charges which they prefer against our people. I do not say that the distinguished Republican gentlemen who have seen fit on this occasion to arraign the people of not only an entire State, but of several States, were actuated by a desire to retain for their tottering party the negro vote in the doubtful Northern States in the pending campaign. I sincerely trust they were actuated by a higher and nobler motive, particularly when we remember that this debate is taking place on the anniversary of the birth of the Father of his Country. . . .

Mr. Chairman, the question raised by the amendment offered by the gentleman from Alabama [Mr. Heflin] is purely a question of disposing of a situation in such manner as will lessen the friction between the races. The adoption of that amendment will not discriminate against the negro race, nor will it inure to the advantage of the white race alone. It will inure to the benefit of both races. It is not intended by the gentleman from Alabama as an attack upon the negro, nor is it an attempt by that gentleman, or by any of us who support it, to deprive the negro of a single right which he has under the law of the land. On its very face it provides equal accommodation for both races on the street cars in the Capital City of this Republic. . . . It is idle to call this amendment a discrimination against the negro. Wherein is the discrimination? The amendment itself contains no discrimination. The language used contains no hint of discrimination, yet gentlemen seize upon it as an excuse to arraign the people of an entire section of this country for alleged wrongs to the negro race. Is this fair? Do gentlemen imagine that even the negro, who has been the willing dupe of the Republican party for all these long years, can be longer deceived by these loud quadrennial protestations of affectionate regard for him?

In the city of Jacksonville, which is in my district and is the largest city in the State of Florida, we have the races separated on the street cars, and the negro is protected in the enjoyment of the portion set apart for his use. Within this month a white man has been dealt with in the courts for violating the city ordinance in refusing to vacate when advised that he was in the section set apart for negroes. . . .

While on this phase of the subject, Mr. Speaker, I desire to refer to the unsupported, bald declarations of gentlemen that negroes are not supplied with accommodations equal to those furnished to white people upon railroads in the South. Why gentlemen will persist in these statements I can not understand. Let me suggest something here that in all probability these gentlemen have never thought of. On our Florida railroads—and I presume it is the same in other Southern States—the cars furnished for negro passengers are just as good as those furnished for white passengers. I am free to admit, however, that they do not long remain as good, as comfortable, and as clean as do those set apart for white passengers. You will not have to search long for the reason of this change. The average negro is perfectly happy when he finds himself eating a watermelon or going on a railroad excursion. The railroad companies in the South cater to this weakness of the negro for riding on trains, and scarcely a week passes in the summer time that a negro excursion is not "pulled off" in every neighborhood. They flock to these excursion trains by thousands and of course the cars set apart for the negroes on the regular passenger trains are used for negro excursions.

Imagine a nice, new passenger coach, packed with dirty, greasy, filthy negroes, down South, in midsummer, and you can readily understand why that car does not long remain as good, as clean, and as desirable as a similar car occupied exclusively by white travelers. It is said of Sam Jones, the great Georgia revivalist, that on one occasion a certain Northern gentleman asked him if there was very much difference in the instincts of a "nigger" and a white man. Sam replied that he didn't know as to that, but of one thing he was absolutely sure, and that was that there was a vast difference in the *"out stinks"* of the two.

For more than forty years, Mr. Chairman, the white people of the South have been taxing themselves to educate negro children, have been building churches for them, and in every conceivable way, with a patience and forbearance never excelled in any age, have struggled along with the stupendous task of elevating and fitting for the duties of citizenship this black mass of ignorant, vicious, and incapable freedmen. I am not wise enough to foretell the end of the problem confronting us. Mr. Lincoln said that this nation could not exist "half slave and half free." I think it is equally true that this nation can not exist *half white* and *half black*. I am very sure that no country having within its borders two distinct races, alien to each other in every essential respect, can long exist with any degree of harmony between the two upon the beautiful theory of perfect equality of all before the law.

The position which we of the South occupy on this question is not one of hostility to the negro. It is one of patriotic love for our own race. We would not destroy the negro, but we would preserve the Caucasian. We will do the black man no harm, and we will not allow him to harm the white man. Members of Congress who are dependent upon a few negro votes in order to retain their seats in this body, a few long-haired negrophilists in various sections of the country, and a lot of short-haired white women who disgrace both their race and sex, may rant of injustice and wrong to the end of time, but they had as well realize now as at any other time that, no matter what the cost or how great the sacrifice, we shall under any and all circumstances maintain the integrity of our race and preserve our civilization.

If God Almighty had intended these two races to be equal, He would have so created them. He made the Caucasian of handsome figure, straight hair, regular features, high brow, and superior intellect. He created the negro, giving him a black skin, kinky hair, thick lips, flat nose, low brow, low order of intelligence, and repulsive features. I do not believe that these differences were the result of either accident or mistake on the part of the Creator. I believe He knew what He was doing, and I believe He did just what He wanted to do.

We believe in God, and we are willing to accept His work just as it fell from His hands. But these people who profess to believe that "a white man may be as good as a negro if the white man behaves himself" are not satisfied with God's work in this regard. They are quite sure that they can make a better job of it than did the Creator, hence we find them attempting to remove the black man from the menial sphere for which he was created, and where he may be useful, to a higher circle for which he is entirely unfitted and where he is perfectly useless.

While there are some people of the classes I have described—and I am quite sure they are to be more pitied than censured—the great masses of the white race from one end of the country to the other have race pride sufficient to forever protest against and resist to the last extremity amalgamation with the negro. . . .

[The gentleman from Kansas, Mr. Campbell] is willing that negro children may attend school and in every way be schoolmates with his children; he is willing that he and his family may attend church with negroes and of course, sit side by side with them in the house of worship; he is willing for himself and family to sit side by side with negroes in street cars and other public conveyances; it is fair to assume that he is perfectly willing that he and his family should travel in the same sleeping cars with negroes, eat at the same table in the same dining car, and be guests at the same hotel, and in all these matters be on terms of the most perfect equality with them; but when the gentleman from Kansas [Mr. Campbell] is brought down to the natural and unavoidable result of such association, viz, intermarriage between the two races, and he is *bluntly*, not to say *cruelly*, asked the question if he "would permit a negro to marry his daughter," we see him flush with indignation and anger, and as the rich red Caucasian blood rushes in violent protest to his face, you hear his eloquent voice ring out above all the noise in this Chamber, "No!"

But Mr. Speaker, if the gentleman from Kansas [Mr. Campbell] persists in maintaining in practice his peculiar theories in this regard, I fear the time may come when his vigorous "No!" may prove ineffectual and futile. The gentleman will find that he can not draw the line when and where he pleases. If the negro boy is as capable of mental and social development to the same extent as is the white boy, if there is really no difference between them except a difference in color, why allow the negro boy every privilege you allow the white boy, and then when you have thoroughly educated him, when you have admitted him to your drawing-rooms, and otherwise have blessed him with a superior culture, draw the line arbitrarily, purely on account of his color, and say to him, "Thus far and no farther." Do you believe you can do this? If this is your policy with the negro, then you do him a most grievous wrong. You invite him to climb the ladder, and you assist him from rung to rung, until you have safely landed him on the one next to the top, and then, without notice, you rudely and suddenly strike him down as he reaches for the goal which you have told him should be his.

Why not tell him the truth in the beginning? Why deceive him? Why longer carry on your game of deception?

The gentleman from New York [Mr. Driscoll] says that we have been allowed to have our own way down South with this question for so long that we have grown "bold" enough to come on the floor of this House and make demands for this kind of legislation. The gentleman uses that word "bold" as though he thought we did not have the right to come here and make demands. We do demand, and we have the right to demand. The blood of the "heroes of the Revolution" flows through our veins; from the Revolution to the present day no foreign foe has ever engaged this Republic in battle that Southern blood has not consecrated every place of conflict; in all our history no foreign foe has ever threatened the flag that we did not rally to its defense. In these emergencies we volunteer, and do not have to be drafted. Yes; we have the right to demand. This is our country, as it was the country of our fathers. The country of the white man, not the home of the mongrel. It will always be the white man's country. If the black man and the yellow man each desire to remain with us, occupying the sphere in life for which God Almighty intended each, let them do so. If not content with that, then let them go elsewhere.

Before closing, Mr. Chairman, I desire to say in this connection that able lawyers in this country who have given a great deal of thought to the subject contend that neither the fourteenth nor the fifteenth amendments to the Constitution of the United States were ever constitutionally proposed or constitutionally adopted, and that as a matter of law and fact the negro has no legal status as a citizen.[1] . . .

---

[1]This idea has been widely accepted by southern segregationists and states' rights advocates throughout the 20th century. It rests upon two facts: that the southern states were not represented in Congress when the amendments were adopted and thus the constitutional requirements of a two-thirds vote was not met; and (2) that the southern states not yet readmitted to the union when the amendments were adopted were coerced into ratifying them as a condition for readmission.

A Defense of
Negro Disfranchisement*

THOMAS W. HARDWICK

The kingpin of segregation was disfranchisement. When southern Negroes lost the right to vote, between 1890 and 1910, they lost the only device they had for protecting themselves and preserving a semblance of the rights ostensibly guaranteed them in Radical Reconstruction. By 1910 only token numbers of Negroes were permitted to vote, and white primary laws restricted those to meaningless general elections. Nevertheless, southern segregationists feared that the elaborate complex of customs, laws, and constitutional provisos by which they had accomplished disfranchisement would not endure. Negroes continued to vote outside the South. Many Northerners and racial reformers never accepted disfranchisement, and neither did the Republican Party, at least not formally. The federal government remained a potential threat to policies which, whatever the language in which they appeared in statute books and state constitutions, clearly violated the intent if not the letter of the 14th and 15th Amendments. In 1915 the Supreme Court declared the "grandfather clause" unconstitutional, and the NAACP legal department had won its first major victory. The following address made in 1908 by Democratic Congressman Thomas W. Hardwick of Georgia, is a typical summary of segregationist arguments against Negro voting. Its purpose was not only to reassure segregationists but also to "educate" Northern critics of segregation and disfranchisement.

In males of voting age the negroes number a little more than 2,000,000 in the entire Union, which is not quite 10 per cent of the total number of males of voting age in the Republic. In the eleven

---

*Reprinted from U.S. *Congressional Record,* Vol. 38, Part 2, 58th Cong., 2nd sess. (Washington, D.C.: U.S. Government Printing Office, January 27, 1904), pp. 1276-78.

Southern States which I have named they number in the aggregate of voting age over 1,500,000, varying from 223,000 in Georgia to 61,000 in Florida, and constituting in the aggregate 36 per cent of the entire voting strength of these States, varying from 57 per cent in Mississippi to 19 per cent in Texas.

These enormous figures and percentages can not fail to impress any thoughtful man with the magnitude of the problem that they suggest and with the colossal interests involved in it. The 12,000,000 white people of the eleven Southern States named have irrevocably, finally, and almost unanimously determined that they will prevent, by every constitutional means in their power, these people from exercising the elective franchise, and within the last few years this determination has crystallized into action, and to-day throughout the South the great bulk of them are not permitted to vote, being debarred by provisions and qualifications varying in the different States—in some by property or educational qualifications, in others by requiring the prepayment of taxes prior to voting, and in still others by Australian ballot laws that require varying degrees of intelligence, while in some of the States two or more of these methods are adopted.

So far as the fifteenth amendment is concerned, it is not believed by the great majority of our best-informed lawyers and jurists who have given careful thought to the subject that any of these provisions violate the fifteenth amendment, and it is undoubtedly true that they have so far stood every test of the courts. . . .

What, then, are the objections to negro suffrage? In the first place, the same objection that applies to all hopeless ignorance, especially when that ignorance is the possession of a people not accustomed to participate in representative government, unacquainted with its institutions, and uninspired by its traditions.

Of the more than a million and a half negro males of voting age, three-fourths of a million of them can neither read nor write. Of Alabama's 181,000, 55.8 per cent are totally illiterate. of Arkansas's 88,000, 40.3 per cent are totally illiterate; of Florida's 61,000, 35.9 per cent are totally illiterate; of Georgia's 223,000, 51.4 per cent are totally illiterate; of Louisiana's 147,000, 58.7 per cent are totally illiterate; of Mississippi's 198,000, 47.5 per cent are totally illiterate; of North Carolina's 127,000, 46.4 per cent are totally illiterate; of Tennessee's 112,000, 41.4 per cent are totally illiterate; of Texas's 137,000, 37 per cent are totally illiterate, and of Virginia's 146,000, 45 per cent are totally illiterate.

These figures speak to you more eloquently than any words I can utter, and when you remember that the test of literacy and illiteracy, upon which these figures are based, is *bare ability to read and write,* you can get an inkling as to what the true condition of this race in the South is on this subject; and when you recall that these are statistics taken after more than thirty years of freedom and education, after the States of the South have taxed themselves to exhaustion,[1] and millions of money have been poured out by generous northern philanthropists, for negro education, you will be no longer amazed that the South has at last rid itself to a large extent of this black mass of density and ignorance, who, in the words of one of the recent governors of my State "neither recognize the sanctity of the ballot nor realize the responsibilities of citizenship."

But it may be contended that, appalling as is the present illiteracy of the negro, he has made wonderful progress in education, considering his comparatively short opportunity, and is every day more rapidly and more thoroughly fitting himself for his duties as a citizen and voter. I concede the premise that he is reducing his illiteracy at a rapid rate, but the conclusion that he is therefore and thereby fitting himself for his duties and responsibilities as a citizen and voter I flatly dispute and believe I can successfully controvert. . . . In 1880, 70 per cent of all the negroes in the Republic were illiterate. In 1890, only 56.8 per cent were illiterate, and in 1900 only 44.6 per cent. In the eleven Southern States the figures are not greatly different from those for the entire nation. . . . This seems to indicate rapid and gratifying progress. It does undoubtedly indicate progress along educational lines, but does it follow that with his increased education the negro has in like proportion progressed in the acquirement and attainment of those civic and moral qualifications that will render him a better citizen and voter?

Let us see. Let us look into that question. From 1880 to 1890 his illiteracy in the South had decreased from 77 per cent to 63 per cent—a marvelous gain, an absolute decrease of 14 per cent and a relative

---

[1]This kind of exaggeration is endemic in segregationist literature. *The Proceedings of the Conference for Education in the South* for 1903, the year before Congressman Hardwick made this address, contained the following summary of southern education by Charles W. Dabney, himself a southerner: "In the Southern states, in schoolhouses costing an average of $276 each, under teachers receiving the average salary of $25 a month, we are giving the children in average attendance 5 cents' worth of education a day for eighty-seven days only in the year." Quoted in C. Vann Woodward, *Origins of the New South* (Baton Rouge: Louisiana State University Press, 1951), p. 400.

decrease of 18 per cent. Yet during this same period his criminality increased in more rapid ratio than his illiteracy decreased. . . .

In 1880 there were in these Southern States 2,480 negro prisoners to the million of negro population. In 1890 there were in these States 3,275 negro prisoners to every 1,000,000 of negro population, an absolute increase of 31 per cent in criminality. Still his illiteracy had in this same decade decreased 14 per cent absolutely and 18 per cent relatively. Again in 1880 relative to the white race, and calculating each race upon the basis of population reduced to equality as between each other, the white constituted 27 per cent of the criminal classes of the South and the blacks 73 per cent. Yet in 1890, calculated on this basis, the whites fell from 27 per cent to 16 per cent, while the negroes advanced from 73 per cent to 84 per cent of the total criminal classes, an absolute increase in criminality on this equalized basis of 11 per cent for the negro and a relative increase of 15 per cent. Yet it must not be forgotten that during this same decade the negro had reduced his illiteracy 14 per cent absolutely and 18 per cent relatively. The Census Bureau has not its criminal statistics compiled for the year 1900, but from 1890 to 1900 the last State reports from the eleven Southern States I have named indicate that these same figures are holding good in that decade.

The conclusion is irresistible that the more you educate the negro the more criminal he becomes.[2] But it may be urged that the negro is unfairly treated in these Southern States; that courts and juries are too prone to look seriously on his faults and to condemn him too hastily and to deal with him too harshly. Let us see. Now, if you will take the criminal statistics from the entire Union and from the different States of the North and different sections of the North and West, you will find that the negro has been punished to a very much greater degree—in other words, is very much more criminal—in the North and West than he has been in the South.

---

[2]The absurdity of Hardwick's logic here is so obvious that comment upon it is perhaps unnecessary. The congressman might just as validly have blamed Negro crime rates on the increase in life expectancy among the race. Any discussion of criminality among Negroes (or whites, either, for that matter) in the late 19th and early 20th centuries must be tenuous at best. Not only was justice for the two races uneven and strongly influenced by race prejudice, but statistics themselves were unevenly reported and thus virtually useless. Certainly they had no validity as Hardwick used them. For recent incisive discussions of this problem, see Marvin E. Wolfgang, *Crime and Race, Conceptions and Misconceptions* (New York: American Jewish Committee, 1964); and Pettigrew, *A Profile of the Negro American* (Princeton: D. Von Nostrand Company, 1964); pp. 136-56.

NUMBER OF NEGRO PRISONERS TO MILLION OF NEGRO INHABITANTS*

	1870	1880	1890
United States	1,621	2,480	3,275
Southern states	1,277	2,142	2,810
Highest southern state	1,757†	4,000 ‡	4,673 ‡
Connecticut	6,360	4,861	5,304
Massachusetts	9,729	5,336	7,213
New York	6,375	7,704	9,783
Illinois	4,966	5,415	7,948
Indiana.	2,581	4,638	5,847
Iowa	2,408	2,896	6,475
Ohio	1,990	3,481	5,645
Minnesota	5,521	3,068	6,000
Michigan	3,696	7,195	7,474
Nebraska.	10,274	10,235	5,490

*From *Eleventh Census, Crime, Pauperism, and Benevolence,* part 2, pages 4 to 10 inclusive.
†Virginia.
‡Texas.

Now, what conclusions are you bound to draw from these figures? There are two. First, that he has not been treated unfairly in the South; and, second, that in the North and West, where he is more educated and less illiterate, he is more criminal. Therefore, as I say, you see everywhere the marvelous spectacle of increased negro criminality and of decreasing negro illiteracy linked together, like Siamese twins, all over this Union. Now, I want to ask this question, and I propound it to every thoughtful, candid man: If it is true that education will not keep the negro from crime, if it is true that decreasing illiteracy does not seem to deter him from criminality, by what extraordinary process of reasoning is the conclusion arrived at that it will make him a better citizen or a better voter? . . .

The next objection I urge to negro suffrage is the almost universal corruptibility of the negro as a voter. There may be exceptions to the rule, more or less numerous in the North and West, and, indeed, a few rare ones in the South, but the rule is that any negro, rich or poor, educated or uneducated, will sell his vote, his chief concern being to obtain the highest possible price for it. I have no statistics to demonstrate this truth, but it needs no demonstration. It is a matter of common knowledge among the people of the South, and I believe this truth is known to people everywhere among whom there are any considerable numbers of negroes, and while I do not positively know it, and hence do not assert it, I surmise very strongly that the gentlemen who have controlled the various national Republican conventions since the negro became a political factor could, if they would, give eloquent evidence in corroboration of it.

The negro, of course, is not solely to blame for this; indeed, he is not even equally to blame with others, for where there is a seller there must be a buyer, and the buyer can not surely be held blameless for his part in such a transaction. . . . From the very nature of the transaction, from its secrecy, from the penalties attached to it, and from the opprobrium incurred by it, it is a transaction rarely susceptible, under ordinary circumstances, of proof, and hence the ordinary penalties usually provided by law can rarely be enforced.

I contend that certain truths that I now propose to state are axiomatic and undeniable. What are these truths? They are these: That the right to vote is not an absolute right that exists for the benefit of the individual, but a great civil and political privilege, conferred or withheld for the benefit of and in the interest of society and good government, and that men who so little appreciate their votes as to sell them ought to be deprived of them forever; and from these propositions I draw the necessary conclusion, in the light of the South's unvarying experience with the negro vote, that the negro ought to be disfranchised.

There is another and, if possible, a still more weighty reason why I oppose negro suffrage. The natural, indeed the irresistible, tendency of political equality is toward social equality. No two races have ever yet lived side by side in anything like equal numbers on terms of political and social equality without amalgamation. All history proclaims the truth of this doctrine, without an exception in any age or in any clime.

Amalgamation being impossible so long as there is a single drop of blood in the veins of a single southern white man, it follows that there can be neither social nor political equality between the races; that so long as they live together there must be the positions of superior and inferior, and that the white race will demand and take the superior position is beyond controversy. Six thousand years of history proclaim his right to it. Superior mental and moral force assert it. Justice and equity unite in confirming his title to it in this land that his adventurous ancestors discovered and conquered from its savage inhabitants, wrested from foreign tyranny, and in which they have founded and preserved that Government that is to-day the richest, the most powerful, and the most glorious on earth.

And who is the negro that he should dispute this demand? A race that never yet founded a government or built a state that did not soon lapse into barbarism; a race that never yet made a single step toward civilization, except under the fostering care and guidance of the white man; a race into whose care was committed one of the three great continents, and who has made it ever since the remotest times a land of utter darkness, until today the nations of Europe, in the onward march of irresistible civilization, are dividing his heritage, the greatest of the continents among themselves. . . .

But it may be asked, what then of the negro; you take from him the ballot that was conferred upon him for the preservation of his freedom and the protection of his civil rights—what substitute do you propose?

The answer is simple. His civil rights are forever secured to him by section 1 of the fourteenth amendment, and so far as the South is concerned I wish to say this, that with his political inferiority established and his social ambition checked he will quietly and peaceably assume that inferior position for which nature and training have fitted him, and so long as he is in their midst the people of the South, who understand him better and treat him more fairly than any other people on earth, and who have for him, in his proper place, a real regard, will see to it that his civil rights are safeguarded and protected—those civil rights that they have never been disposed to deny him since his emancipation, the right to have a fair and impartial trial in the courts, to labor when and where he pleases without abuse or molestation, the security of personal liberty, and the preservation of private property, as well as assistance to material progress and encouragement to the cultivation of those civic virtues that adorn every good citizen, high or low, and whose absence is a reproach to the mightiest.

The objection may be made that this system proposes to tax him without giving him a voice in the Government. The answer is that taxation and the right to vote have never been coincident in any government, and have never been in this Government. Is a negro man better than a white woman? Yet you tax the woman who owns property and in only two or three States out of forty-five do you permit her to vote.

The objection may be made that this system denies the elective franchise to the negro, and yet military service may be required of him. The answer is that military service and the right to vote have never gone hand in hand, even in this Government. Boys between 18 and 21 years of age are subject to military service, and yet they are not permitted to vote, and men over 45 years of age are exempt from military service, and yet they are permitted to vote. . . .

I am not without hope, even under ordinary conditions, as to the ultimate success of the cause I advocate to-day. I can not despair when I recall that not many months have passed since the Republican Secretary of War, Mr. Root, addressing this same Union League Club in New York City, admitted that the experiment of negro suffrage had failed and that the country must realize its failure and prepare to consider next what new remedy could be proposed for existing conditions.

I can not despair when not many months have elapsed since the New York Sun, one of the greatest and most influential papers in the nation, Republican in its politics, but a brave, independent paper, with convictions of its own—and it is not afraid to express them— admits the tremendous mistake that was made in 1869 and 1870, and plainly says that "sooner or later the country will have to face the question of the repeal of the fifteenth amendment, and perhaps the sooner the better for the dignity of the instrument, which exhibits as a fundamental principle of the American system a theory of suffrage impossible of practical application with safety to the vital interests of the States chiefly concerned;" when this view of the matter seems to be indorsed by such widely read journals as Harper's Weekly, the Public Ledger of Philadelphia, the Providence Journal, and a large number of other northern and western papers and magazines; when this view is advocated and supported by such well-known sociologists as Prof. Leon Prince, Prof. Jerome Dowd, Prof. Goldwin Smith, Mr. A. R. Colquhoun, Rev. Dr. Parkhurst, and others.

Well has it been suggested that it is the most brazen of inconsistencies for the National Government to guarantee the suffrage to black men in the South while it denies it to brown men in the Philippines and to white men in Porto Rico.

Christian Principles
and the Race Issue*

THEODORE DuBOSE BRATTON

Not all segregationists are extremists or demagogues. In the years since 1890, many (maybe most) of them have been moderates who consider themselves friends of the Negro, and have in fact often endorsed measures to uplift the race. Critical of the extremist and the demagogue, these moderates are often strongly influenced by religion, and consider Christianity the best guide to racial policy and interracial conduct. But in spite of their well-meaning endeavors, moderates, especially those in the South, have themselves generally been white supremacists. Before 1954, southern moderates almost invariably endorsed segregation and restrictions on Negro voting. They proposed no fundamental change in southern race policy; instead, they hoped to eliminate the harsher aspects of white supremacy and neutralize its most brutal consequences. Their discussion of racial topics was positive and optimistic in tone, but also naive, and, one might add, unreal, even deluded. They seem to believe that a generous portion of positive thinking would solve a desperate problem. The principles of Jesus Christ, they intoned, are the only hope for either race.

These features of what was a major element of segregationist thought are illustrated in the following address by Episcopal Bishop Theodore DuBose Bratton to the 1908 Conference for Education in the South. Bishop Bratton, of Jackson, Mississippi, was active in numerous racial uplift causes, and his address indicates that moderates and "uplifters" were themselves an obstacle to Negro equality. Through "Christian education" Bratton would teach Negroes to accept segregation and subordination, and make themselves more useful

---

*Reprinted from Theodore DuBose Bratton, "The Christian South and Negro Education," *Sewanee Review*, Vol. XVI (July, 1908), pp. 290-97.

and acceptable to the white man. Thus education, religion, and racial moderation itself furthered the cause of white supremacy. Well might Negroes complain that with friends like the Bishop, who needs enemies!

"The Christian South." A word about it. The South above any other section represents Anglo-Saxon America, native-born America. Scarcely more than a trace of foreign born is to be found in the Southern States. Our people are born into American ideals and conditions and reflect Anglo-Saxon traditions of home and family. That they are Christian (after our human fashion and in the measure of present human ability) no one is better able to attest than a bishop who goes in and out among every class of his fellows. Should this great body of Anglo-Americans ever cease to be Christian, or become less Christian than it is, the effect upon our entire nation would be disastrous beyond the power of thought to conceive. That it should become more and more Christian in thought and practice is not only devoutly to be wished, but is inexpressibly important to the necessarily progressive settlement of the gravest question, in its deep and wide moral effects, before the mind and heart of the American people. . . . It is [not?] too much to say that the "race issue" is more vitally intermingled with those essential problems whose solution affects the moral life and therefore the peace, prosperity and happiness of America than any other one issue in social life. And the solution, if it is ever to be worked out at all, is going to be found through the Christian thought and sentiment and the labor of Christian men of science.

I am one of those who believe that God is the God of nations, and that Jesus Christ our Lord is the light as well as the life of man; that no issue is settled without His guidance; that all issues may be settled with it. The real key to the answer of life's problems without is to be found in the solved problems within. The real solution of the vexed and vexing issues of social life is, and always has been, found in the growth of men's minds in the knowledge of God and of God's laws, and of His methods of dealing with life. Whatever the Christian South may do practically, however far short of the ideal she may find it necessary to fall from time to time in meeting practical difficulties, however clouded by political issues this ideal of Christian and democratic relationship of races may be, she cannot blind her eyes to that which the Christ has set, the ideal of a Christian life which expresses itself in work, in forbearance, in unfailing hope.

It is not by accident that the negro is in our midst, that Anglo-Saxon America of to-day has inherited the problem (greater than that of our fathers) of his relation to his white neighbor. It is not by accident that he has learned from the whites the ambition to rise and the inspiration to higher life intellectual and moral. These are the outcome, not of accident, but of Divine Providence. And they constitute one of those opportunities of national life, the issue of which is the Nation's judgment. The more I study the great problem the less able am I to see the end of its progressive solution. Only a few things seem to me to stand out clearly and distinctly above the dust clouds.

First, That the negro is capable of development to a point whose limit I have not yet discovered.

Second, That the vast majority are still children intellectually and little short of savage morally.

Third, That the relation between the races at present, however theoretically estranged, is yet practically and very largely kindly, cordial, and often affectionate—only really disturbed by the astonishingly small class of brutes whose diabolical conduct acts as fire to combustibles.

Fourth, That whatever the future may have in store, the present has the grave duty of making better the generation with which it has to deal, and the certain result of aiding the future solution through the training of more enlightened and moral and responsible characters who will grapple with the problem. No one will be hardy enough to maintain that ignorance is as wise as enlightenment, or that the one is as safe as the other.

Fifth, That no solution of difficulties growing out of the relations of two races is going to be permanent and satisfactory unless both races have made contributions to it. For no arbitrary solution, imposed from without,[1] is either apt to be right, or likely to be tolerated for long.

This brings me to the final consideration for which all that I have said has been preparing—the education of the negro. The only right way to help a race, or an individual (unless he be an invalid or an

---

[1] "Without" here refers to the North and the federal government. Earlier in his address, the Bishop had been critical of Radical Reconstruction and of Radical efforts to help the freedmen.

imbecile), is to help him help himself, and this, in its wide sense, is education. Education does not mean Latin and Greek and mathematics and literature; it does not mean one or all of these things in the education of some exceptional being. But to train the mind to right uses of its powers, that it may do its duty in discriminating absorption of what life and experience offer to it, rejecting the meretricious and assimilating and incorporating the meritorious into its life, and thus to edify the character—this is the business of education. The success, of course, depends largely upon the discriminating ability of the teacher, who studies his pupil as closely as he does the subjects to be imparted.

I say of this education, of this helping the negro to help himself, that it is the duty of the Christian South (which she has been fulfilling right nobly, too), that it is necessary to the welfare of our land, to the better development of both races, and to their more peaceful relations. Do not misunderstand me; I do not propose education as the solution, and the only solution, of the great problem. I propose it as an auxiliary force in its solution incalculably strong. I propose it as the divine power which is instinct with the religion which God gave to His people in the olden time, and which He immeasurably enlarged in Jesus Christ our Lord, by which He would lead His people out of darkness into light. Religion is in a real sense education, in my thought of it; it presupposes it and requires it as a necessary corollary. And the religion of the Christ, Who is the light of men, is unthinkable without the divine illumination of all God's mysteries, natural and spiritual, human and divine, earthly and heavenly.

Of all the races with whom we come in contact, the negro certainly does not need less than others this education which is to take account of all his faculties, and both of his natures, the natural and the spiritual. The fact that he lives in the midst of enlightenment dooms him the more surely to deterioration unless his faculties be trained. And who can doubt but that his deterioration must drag down the great body of those who are in closest relation to him?

. . . If this be the education needed to meet conditions, who is to provide it? It is easily conceivable that the time will come when the development of the choicest spirits among the negroes will provide the prophets of both religion and enlightenment to their race. But I do not believe that any one who knows the race in its present stage of development would venture to say that it is wise to leave it entirely to its own leadership in any department of life. I would not detract one iota from the distinction (which I rejoice in) which any of the great negro leaders have achieved, but, in my judgment, the negroes are not yet ready to emancipate themselves wholly from white guidance and white leadership. The ideal educational work among the race is being done more largely by schools which are under white management and instruction than by those under the control of negroes alone. . . . There is another and perhaps a deeper reason for my contention for white supervision of negro education. The negro's life must be lived among the whites. The adjustments of life are not always easy to be made. The estrangements would be intolerable if they became extreme to the point of hatred. And, however the better and more cultured class of negroes would express it to themselves, some similar thought is in their minds when they, too, many of them, are anxious that the separation of the races shall not extend to the point of all loss of contact with white teacher or preacher. . . .

[Negroes] need the help of . . . white people. If I were able to establish what I consider the ideal school to meet our conditions . . . , this is what I would have. A rural industrial plant, with perhaps a clergyman of practical abilities, or certainly a devoutly religious layman, at its head; with the [Apostles'] Creed, the Lord's Prayer, the Ten Commandments, the Sermon on the Mount, as necessary parts of the curriculum, just as necessary as spelling or plowing; with morality as the foundation of everything; an institution segregated from town temptation,[2] where discipline would be firmly, rigidly and kindly enforced; where the arts of nature could be taught and God in His nature studied, known and loved; where the race would be taught that race integrity is obedience to God's own creation and appointment, and race intercourse, kindly and cordial, is not race equality; that indeed "race equality," the very expression, is an anachronism belonging to . . . Reconstruction history, which is gone long ago to its reckoning; that there is no use of such expressions as race equality as between white and black any more than between white and yellow. They are simply two races living in the same

---

[2]Segregationists, whether moderates or extremists, generally agreed in the early 20th century that the proper place for Negroes was in the South and on the farm. They believed Negroes were best suited by training and ability to farming, and the southern agricultural system offered the ideal means of assisting—and controlling—the race. Adherents to the agrarian myth, segregationists considered towns and cities to be centers of vice and corruption, places where interracial contacts were often casual and sometimes improper, where Negroes lost their sense of deference and became "uppity" and dissatisfied.

territory and trying to be as helpful to one another as possible and trying to work out God's great problem as best they can. The races of men are equally the great God's children, and their destiny is in His hands. The purpose of race distinction is known only to Him. Much, no doubt, can be learned of His purpose through the research of consecrated Christian men of scientific mind working in union, and above all, working in true scientific spirit to discover God's purpose for His creation. No other spirit will reveal the truth concerning this great question.

A Segregationist on Negro Militancy*

JAMES F. BYRNES

World War I had a profound impact upon race relations in the United States. Negroes as well as whites imbibed the exalted rhetoric of the crusade to make the world safe for democracy. Not surprisingly, many of them concluded that what is good for the world is good for America. Race relations, they began to insist, should be restructured on a democratic basis. Negroes should have equal rights, opportunities, and responsibilities; segregation and disfranchisement must be abolished. More than 350,000 Negroes served in the armed forces during the war, and even larger numbers migrated to the cities of northern and border states to work in war-related industries. The war thus created a new environment for many Negroes and helped awaken them to the possibility of better treatment for their race. After the war, they were little inclined to accept old patterns of race relations, and the result was a new militancy among Negroes which produced a strong and sometimes violent reaction among segregationists. In 1919, the nation endured its first "long, hot summer." Significant outbursts of racial violence occurred in Washington, Chicago, Knoxville, Omaha, and Elaine, Arkansas, and lesser outbursts in a dozen and more areas scattered across the nation. The following address by James F. Byrnes, then a young congressman from South Carolina, reflects the segregationist's reaction to this wave of racial violence and to increasing Negro militancy. Congressman Byrnes, one of the most important political figures of the 20th-century South, was later a U.S. Senator, Associate Justice of the Supreme Court, Secretary of State, and governor of South Carolina. His address indicates that neither the demands of Negro militants nor the response of segregationists to those demands has changed much during the last half century.

*Reprinted from U.S. *Congressional Record*, Vol. 58, Part 5, 66th Cong., 1st sess. (Washington, D.C.: U.S. Government Printing Office, August 25, 1919), pp. 4303-05.

The recent race riots in Washington and Chicago, and the many other similar disturbances throughout the country, have caused much speculation in the press as to the underlying causes of the conflict between the races. It is manifest that when sanguinary conflicts take place in cities so widely separated and within so short a time the cause is general and not local. Those who read the newspapers of the country know that there has been no propaganda to arouse the antagonism of the white man toward the negro. On the contrary, the very generous support of the war by the negro caused the white people of the Nation to entertain for him only the best of good feeling. For this sudden change in our relations, then, we must look to negro leadership to ascertain whether or not efforts have been made to disturb the harmonious relations heretofore existing in this country. The *New York Times* of August 5 carried a statement quoting Dr. L. B. Moore, dean of Howard University (negro), as saying that—

A well-trained teacher in one of our larger schools of the South told me that the colored people were being organized by representatives of the I.W.W., and we are in danger of having a little Russia in many sections of the South.[1]

Coming from South Carolina, I think I know something of the negro, and I am convinced that there is little foundation for the opinion expressed by the dean of Howard University. In the South to-day the negro is prospering as never before in the history of his race. He is accumulating money, he is purchasing land, and through the assistance of the white man is daily bettering his condition. Left to ourselves there is no possibility of conditions arising in the South which would justify the description of a "little Russia."

But the statement above quoted, together with the general speculation as to the cause of the riots in Washington and Chicago, has caused me to inquire into the attitude of the negro press, and I have become convinced that the race antagonism manifesting itself throughout the country is due to the incendiary utterances of the would-be leaders of the race now being circulated through negro newspapers and magazines. It is evident that the leadership of [Robert R.] Moton

---

[1]The Russian Revolution of 1917 injected a new element into segregationist thought. It provided segregationists with an explanation of racial unrest which completely absolved themselves of blame. Segregationists refused to believe Negroes, especially those in the South, were dissatisfied with segregation. Negro militancy must therefore have other causes. It *must* result from "outside agitation" and some form of diabolical conspiracy. Only international communism or "the Bolsheviki of Russia" could account for such a widespread campaign, so Byrnes believed. The Industrial Workers of the World (IWW), a syndicalist-socialist labor union organized in 1905, was often described by segregationists as the source of racial unrest before World War I.

and others, who, following in the steps of Booker Washington, preached conservatism to the race, is now being challenged by a crowd of radicals who are appealing to the passions of the negroes and inciting them to deeds of violence. These radical leaders are urging their followers to resort to violence in order to secure privileges they believe themselves entitled to, and the recent riots indicate that many are accepting this bad advice. It is unfortunate that some negro leaders heretofore regarded as conservative have changed their attitude.

A fair illustration of this type is W. E. B. Du Bois, editor of the *Crisis Magazine*. Du Bois has heretofore rendered great service to his people by intelligent leadership. He has acquired influence over many thoughtful negroes, and therefore his capacity for evil is enlarged. The recent issues of his magazine are filled with appeals to the prejudice and the passions of the negro, which can have no other result than to incite him to deeds of violence. A fair example is an editorial in the May issue of the *Crisis,* page 13, where, under the headlines "Returning soldiers," he declares:

We sing: This country of ours, despite all its better souls have done and dreamed, is yet a shameful land.

It lynches. . . . It disfranchises its own citizens. . . . It encourages ignorance. . . . It steals from us. . . . It insults us.

To support each one of these statements he prints a short argument, concluding with the following:

This is the country to which we soldiers of democracy return. This is the fatherland for which we fought! But it is our fatherland. It was right for us to fight. The faults of our country are our faults. Under similar circumstances we would fight again. But by the God of heaven we are cowards and jackasses if now that the war is over we do not marshall every ounce of our brain and brawn to fight a sterner, longer, more unbending battle against the forces of hell in our land.

We return.

We return from fighting.

We return fighting.

Make way for democracy! We saved it in France; and by the great Jehovah, we will save it in America or know the reason why.

The espionage law still in force provides that one who shall willfully print, write, or publish any language intended to incite, provoke, or encourage resistance to the United States, or who shall publish any abusive language about the form of government of the

United States, shall be punished by a fine or imprisonment. If this editorial, which refers to this as a "shameful land," charging the Government with lynching, disfranchising its citizens, encouraging ignorance, and stealing from its citizens, does not constitute a violation of the espionage law, it is difficult to conceive language sufficiently abusive to constitute a violation. Believing this to be true, I have called this editorial to the attention of the Attorney General, with the request that if in the judgment of his department it does constitute a violation of the law, that proceedings be instituted against Du Bois. No greater service can be rendered to the negro today than to have him know that this Government will not tolerate on the part of a leader of his race action which constitutes a violation of the law and which tends to array the negro race against the Government under which they live and under which the race has made greater strides than it has under any other Government on earth. [Applause.]

The same issue of the *Crisis,* on page 20, carries, with the apparent approval of its editor, a letter written by a negro officer in France, containing this statement:

I am beginning to wonder whether it will ever be possible for me to see an American (white) without wishing that he were in his Satanic Majesty's private domain. I must pray long and earnestly that hatred of my fellow man be removed from my heart, and that I can truthfully lay claim to being a Christian.

As one can not well enter his Satanic Majesty's private domain until after death, his statement simply means that he wishes every American—white—was dead and in hell. His wish is qualified in no way. It applies alike to the white man of the North and of the South. And to think that this man was honored by his country with a commission as an officer of the United States Army! That his view is shared by other negroes who served as officers in the Army is evident from the statements of one William N. Colson, a contributing editor to the *Messenger,* another negro magazine. Colson claims to have been an officer in the Three hundred and sixty-seventh Infantry. In the July issue of the *Messenger,* under the headline "Propaganda and the American negro soldier," he writes:

A feeble and indefinite propaganda did spring up among the negro soldiers in France. In that democratic clime they found themselves. They felt better within themselves because they were fighting for France and for their race rather than for a flag which had no meaning.

I regret that any man for whom our flag had no meaning ever "found himself" in France or elsewhere in the uniform of an officer of the Army of the United States.

He tells us:

No intelligent American negro is willing to lay down his life for the United States as it now exists.

Again:

Intelligent negroes have all reached the point where their loyalty to the country is conditional.

I certainly hope that this does not accurately state the attitude of the intelligent negroes of America. But this man tells us, further:

The consensus of opinion among thinking colored people is that the war ended too soon. They believe that the American negro would have gotten a status had America been chastised more severely.

In other words, they regret, according to this ex-officer, that more of our boys were not forced to die in France. And in the August issue of the *Messenger,* this same officer, under the heading "An analysis of negro patriotism," writes:

The negro soon found that the treachery of the white American was infinitely more damaging to him than the Hun.

When black officers taught black men bayonet practice they usually substituted the picture of the rabid white southerner for that of the Hun. This method often inspired the soldier with the necessary dash and form.

The colored officer, maltreated and thrust aside, has cursed the flag and the country for which it stands a thousand times. Thousands of these soldiers now possess weapons to demonstrate, if need be, their legal right to self-defense against southern encroachments and lynch law.

. . . For criticism of our Government and of our flag, much less severe than the above statements, many white men were placed in jail during the last two years. Peace has not been proclaimed, and I do not see why this man should escape prosecution. The fact that he is a colored man should not entitle him to any special privilege. Having held a commission as an officer in the Army, he should be held to a stricter accountability than the man who was not so honored. I am loath to believe that he expresses the views of the intelligent negroes of America, but his uncontradicted statements should receive careful consideration from those who have looked with favor upon the organization of additional negro regiments with negro officers.

A possible explanation of the feeling of these negro officers is contained on page 21 of the May issue of the *Crisis,* where complaint is made that the issuance of an order prevented them from attending a dance where they could dance with white women. . . .

When Du Bois is guilty of publishing stuff of this kind, it is not surprising to find William Monroe Trotter, editor of the *Boston Guardian* (negro), doing his utmost to incite riots and cause bloodshed. The *New York Times* of July 28 quotes him as stating in a speech made the day previous:

I told them in Paris that unless and until a concerted guaranty were given of citizenship based upon full democracy, with no distinction as to race or color, there could be no world peace, and in the same week of my arrival home my heart is made to swell within me because the new spirit of my own race taught the world that they refused to be shot down in the capital of Lincoln. While they were degrading us they were making our boys fight for them. Unless the white American behaves, he will find that in teaching our boys to fight for him he was starting something that he will not be able to stop.

. . . On the same day these statements were made the blacks began their destructive work in Chicago.

Trotter, in addressing an audience at the Metropolitan M.E. Church in Washington last week [after the riot], declared, according to the *Washington Eagle* (negro) of August 16:

Washington was saved from a dreadful disgrace when the colored men were not driven out of the city, which was the ultimate aim of the white brutes. If it were the lawless element of our race that stopped the onslaught, then the others of us should hang our heads in disgrace. We have shown how we can, and will retaliate. The other race will think twice the next time before they strike a single blow. Innocent pedestrians were maltreated near the doors of the White House, while the President stood inside. Washington papers did all they could to stir up race antagonism. It was the fighting qualities of the negro who stayed in the streets that put an end to the trouble.

In his speech he also stated:

A new negro is facing the white man to-day—one who has been aroused by a consecutive number of insults. Instead of replying "Yes, dear sir," and "No, dear sir," a sharp "Indeed" or "Yes" is heard, as the case may be. There will be no peace until the White Americans learn to respect the rights of colored Americans.

. . . While these publications and the *Challenge,* edited by William Bridges, vie with each other in the publications of such incendiary stuff as I have read, the *Messenger,* edited by A. Philip Randolph and Chandler Owen, boasts that it is the only radical negro magazine in America, and does its utmost to prove that it is at least the most radical negro publication. It is printed upon paper of fine quality. It does not carry a half dozen advertisements other than its own advertisements, and it is evident that it is supported by contributions from some source. The material in the magazine would indicate that the source from which the support comes is antagonistic to the Government of the United States. It appeals for the establishment in this country of a Soviet government. It praises the treatment of the negro by the Germans as contrasted with the treatment accorded the negro by the allied forces. It urges the negro to join the I.W.W.'s; pays tribute to Debs and every other convicted enemy of the Government, and prays for the establishment of a Bolsheviki government in this land. It is evident that the I.W.W.'s are financing it in an effort to have the negro of America join them in their revolutionary plans. Under the headline, "Why negroes should join the I.W.W.," it states that 149,000 negroes engaged in railroad transportation do not belong to the Brotherhood organizations, and by joining the I.W.W.'s they could tie up the railroads as completely as could the Big Four Brotherhoods. Under the heading, "Negro police captains," the *Messenger* urges that negroes be made police captains in all large cities, and with a rare gift of prophecy announced in the July issue:

All such big negro communities are magazines of race prejudice dynamite, ready to explode at any moment upon putting the flame to the fuse. Riots are imminent—real race riots—in all such large cities as New York, Philadelphia, Baltimore, Washington, Chicago, Pittsburgh, and St. Louis.

. . . Since the publication of this magazine most unfortunate race riots have occurred in Washington and Chicago. In determining who was the aggressor, the above statements are enlightening. They show that the negro leaders had deliberately planned a campaign of violence. . . .

Now, let us see the nature of the appeal to which the negro is said to be giving an ear. On page 10 of the August issue of the *Messenger* you will find the following:

At the present time two forms of attack will suffice for negroes to enter upon. Whenever you hear talk of a lynching a few hundred of you must assemble rapidly and let the authorities know that you propose to have them abide by the law and not violate it. Offer your services to the mayor or the governor, pledging him that you can protect the life of any prisoner if the State militia has no such power. Ask the governor or the authorities to supply you with additional arms, and under no circumstances should you southern negroes surrender your arms, for lynching mobs to come in and have sway. To organize your work a little more effectively, get in touch with all the negroes who were in the draft. Form little voluntary companies, which may quickly be assembled. Find negro officers who will look after their direction. Be perfectly calm, poised, cool, and self-contained. Do not get excited, but face your work with cold resolution, determined to uphold the law and protect the lives of your fellows at any cost. When this is done nobody will have to sacrifice his life or that of anybody else, because nobody is going to be found who will try to overcome that force. . . .

I will not burden you with further quotations from the negro press. These are sufficient to advise you of the evil forces at work. If upon the statute books there is now no law prohibiting the circulation through the mails of incendiary doctrines such as I have cited, then it is time that legislation is enacted to prohibit it. We can all believe in a free press, but we can recognize the distinction between a free press and a revolutionary, an anarchistic press. For a long time we failed to realize the danger of permitting the publication of revolutionary doctrines in the foreign-language press. To-day they are under close surveillance, and in like manner we should now prevent the I.W.W. and the Bolsheviki of Russia from using the negro press of America to further their nefarious purposes.

I call these quotations from the negro press to the attention of the white men of America in order that they may know of the efforts that are being made to induce the negro to resort to violence.

I call attention to the statements of the negro press for the further purpose of expressing the hope that among the negro leaders there are men who care more for the future of their race than they do for their own personal ambition, and who will tell their people that in seeking political and social equality they are cherishing false hopes and are doomed to disappointment.

If the two races are to live together in this country it may as well be understood that the war has in no way changed the attitude of the white man toward the social and political equality of the negro. If as a result of his experience in the war he does not care to live in this land without political and social equality, then he can depart for any other country he wishes, and his departure will be facilitated by the white people of this country, who desire no disturbing factor in their midst. If by reason of his experience he seeks social and political equality with the white man, but refuses to consider leaving for parts where it will be willingly given to him, and cherishes the hope that by violence it can be gained here, he can not too quickly realize that there are in this country 90,000,000 white people determined not to extend political and social equality to the 10,000,000 negroes, and a resort to violence must inevitably bring to the negro the greater suffering.

If there is left in the race any sane leadership it should now be exerted to counteract the evil effects of the radicals. The negro must realize that his progress is dependent upon the assistance of the white man with whom he lives. In the South, where, in the opinion of up-lifters, the negro is ill treated, the truth is that the negro is making rapid progress. He is accumulating money; he is buying property and educating his children. He lives in better homes and often travels in automobiles. His business opportunities are practically unlimited. He is protected in his life and property. He is happy and contented and will remain so if the propagandist of the I.W.W., the Bolsheviki of Russia, and the misguided theorist of other sections of this country will let him alone. I know that whenever a lynching takes place in the South it is heralded to the country as an evidence of barbaric oppression of the negro. Mob law is always indefensible and inexcusable. In the South lynchings are condemned by the press, the pulpit, and by public men who unceasingly urge reliance upon the courts. But not-withstanding all efforts, the fact is that whenever a negro commits an assault upon a white woman the white man does not reason. He acts. And only extraordinary efforts on the part of law officials will prevent lynching.

I know that lynchings have occurred for provocations other than criminal assault, but I know, too, of many instances where law officers have died protecting prisoners against mob violence. I know that men who participated in lynchings have been convicted, and the law-abiding people of the South are doing their utmost to bring about a sentiment of upholding the law under all circumstances. But in miti-gation rather than defense of the South in this matter it must be said that the mob very rarely, if ever, does violence to any but the guilty negro. It has never used the provocation of one criminal negro as an excuse for recklessly assailing the law-abiding negroes of the com-munity. The mob may lynch the guilty man, but the law-abiding negro knows he is in no danger.

Another peculiar thing is that while the press of the North and the negro press will join the press and pulpit of the South in their condemnation of the criminality of the mob, they seldom join us in condemnation of the criminal assaults upon white women, which is generally the cause of the lynching.[2]

Recently the Chicago newspapers asked the governors of the various Southern States whether employment could be provided for southern negroes who had recently gone to Chicago. The South can provide employment for every law-abiding negro who wishes to return. But for any negro who has become inoculated with the desire for political equality or social equality there is no employment in the South, nor is there any room for him in the South.

It is stated that most of the negroes who went to Chicago from the Southern States during the last few years were induced to go by employment leagues, who held out to them the hope of higher wages, better conditions, and social equality. The *Chicago News,* two days prior to the race riot, stated that each of these employment leagues published a newspaper which circulated in the South setting forth the advantage of conditions in that city. It is suggested that behind this propaganda was the desire of some politicians to enlarge their political influence by increasing the number of negro voters and the desire on the part of some capitalists to secure in the negro a prospective strike breaker and a lever to keep down the wages of the workingman. Whatever was the inspiration, the effect of the emigration of the negro to Northern States has been to make the negro problem a national instead of a sectional one.

It has been said that "the North has the principles, but the South has the negroes." To-day the North also has the negro, and with the coming of the negro many of its theories have departed. People of the North have come to realize that in the absence of daily contact with the negro they could believe in political and social equality of the races, but that whenever the negroes in any large number come into a community or State that belief is swept away by that which is greater than constitutional or legislative enactments, namely, the

---

[2]Byrnes' comments on lynching were typical of those which appear in segregationist literature, especially his statement that lynchings are "generally" caused by the rape or attempted rape of white women by Negro men. Professor Thomas F. Gossett wrote recently of lynching: "In 1942, a study of lynching disclosed that of the 3,811 Negroes lynched between 1889 and 1941, only 641, or less than 17 per cent, were even accused of rape, either attempted or committed. Negroes were lynched for such 'crimes' as threatening to sue a white man, attempting to register to vote, enticing a white man's servant to leave his job, engaging in labor union activities, 'being disrespectful to' or 'disputing with' a white man, or sometimes for no discoverable reason at all. Mary Turner, in Georgia, was hanged and burned when she was almost at the point of childbirth because she threatened to disclose the names of the men who had killed her husband." Thomas F. Gossett, *Race: The History of an Idea in America* (Dallas: Southern Methodist University Press, 1963), p. 270.

natural instinct of the Anglo-Saxon. No better evidence of this truth can be asked than the changed attitude of the northern press. For years the *Chicago Tribune* led the press of the North in criticism of the South because of its attitude toward the negro. It is interesting to-day to read in its editorial columns the following:

> We are swiftly getting to the point where our colored citizens must look the facts in the face. There will be no political injustice. There will be social differences. They need not be unjust. They do exist, and they will. The thinking negroes must use their influence with their race. They must realize the facts and conditions.

This ardent champion of negro rights now declares there will be social differences, and thus sustains the position of the white man of the South. They state, "There will be no political injustice." If by that is meant there will be no restriction of the exercise of the franchise by the negro, then I say to them that if they are honest they will say there will be no restriction in any community where the whites have an overwhelming majority. But I know that just as soon as in any northern community the negroes increase in number to such an extent as to endanger the political control of the white man, just so soon will there be restriction of his right to vote, because this is a white man's country, and will always remain a white man's country. So much for political equality.

As to social equality, God Almighty never intended that a white race and a black race should live on terms of social equality, and that which the Creator did not intend man can not make possible.

Neither political equality nor social equality is essential to the happiness of the negro. The population of the congressional district I represent is about evenly divided between the races. In one county, however, there are seven or eight negroes to one white man, and, parenthetically, I might say that in that county there is less race trouble than in any county of the State. I know the negroes of my district do not seek to participate in politics. I know that they do not seek social equality. I know they do seek to better their condition and that the white man is daily aiding them in their progress. I know that if left alone they will continue contented, and I do not want these radical negro publications, whether supported by the I.W.W., the Bolsheviki of Russia, or the misguided theorist of the North, to be circulated among them, arousing the passions of the criminal class of negroes, and resulting in injury to the law-abiding negro as well as to the white people of the South. [Applause]

A Segregationist Discusses Interracial Marriage*

J. THOMAS HEFLIN

Whatever the intensity of their racial views, all segregationists and white supremacists looked upon intermarriage with horror. Upon this issue moderates joined ranks with the most outspoken bigots and demagogues. The number of interracial marriages was never significant, though apparently there was always a considerable amount of illicit amalgamation. The latter was ritually denounced by segregationists, but never with such ardor or at such great length as the former. Segregationists, especially those in politics and public life, thrive on emotion, and intermarriage was an ideal subject for their harangues. No discussion of the race issue by one of them was complete without reference to the issue, often accompanied by warnings that widespread intermarriage was imminent. The following letter (and ensuing remarks) from Alabama Senator J. Thomas Heflin, one of the South's most notorious and bigoted segregationists, is typical of the extremists' reaction to interracial marriages.

Washington, D.C., October 15, 1929

Mr. Sam H. Reading
  National News Service,
    24 North Fifty-ninth Street, Philadelphia, Pa.

My Dear Sir: In reply to your request I will say that I have read with a feeling of sadness and indignation the newspaper account of the humiliated and grief-stricken white father and mother in New York

---

*Reprinted from U.S. *Congressional Record*, Vol. 72, Part 3, 71st Cong., 2nd sess. (Washington, D.C.: U.S. Government Printing Office, 1929), pp. 3234-3239.

123

City who could get no assistance from either Governor Roosevelt or Mayor Walker or anyone else in authority in their effort to prevent the marriage of their daughter to a negro. The press reports tell us that the white father and mother wept freely when interviewed by the newspaper men and made no attempt to hide their tears and humiliation when New York officials issued a marriage license to a negro to marry their daughter. And this terrible thing has happened here in what we used to call the land of Anglo-Saxon rule and white supremacy. Shame on those in authority who will permit such a humiliating, disgraceful, and dangerous thing to happen in the United States. Where are the white men of self-respect, of race pride, and love of the white man's country in America whose brave forbears long ago decreed that there should be no pollution of the blood of the white race by permitting marriage between whites and negroes? What has become of the brave knights of the white race who once boasted of their proud Caucasian lineage? For many generations they stood guard on the dividing line between the Caucasian race and the Negro race.

The far-reaching harm and danger of marriage between whites and negroes to the great white race that God intended should rule the world is apparent to all intelligent students of history; such mixtures have always resulted in weakening, degrading, and dragging down the superior to the level of the inferior race. God had a purpose in making four separate and distinct races. The white, the red, the yellow, and the black. God intended that each of the four races should preserve its blood free from mixture with other races and preserve race integrity and prove itself true to the purpose that God had in mind for each of them when He brought them into being.[1] The great white race is the climax and crowning glory of God's creation. God in His infinite wisdom has clothed the white man with the elements and the fitness of dominion and rulership, and the history of the human race shows that wherever he has planted his foot and unfurled the flag of his authority he has continued to rule. No true member of the great white race in America is going to approve or permit, if he can prevent it, the marriage between whites and negroes.

---

[1]This line of reasoning is often used by segregationists in opposing racial intermarriage. However, it might be contended that segregationists applied their logic to only one-half the issue. God obviously had a plan in creating separate races, they argued; not one of them, however, ever speculated upon the Almighty's purpose in making it possible for the races to interbreed and produce fertile offspring.

This desire and purpose on the part of the great white race in America to keep its blood strain pure and to prevent marriage between whites and negroes can better be designed as the "call of the blood." It has come down to us through the centuries. White women, rather than become the wives of the black man, whenever the issue was presented, fought and died, if necessary, to remain true to the "call of the blood." But it seems that in New York, under alien influence, that the line of demarcation between the great white race and the Negro race, the "great divide," that once constituted the "dead line" in America on questions of social equality and marriage between whites and negroes, have been repudiated by those of the Roman-Tammany regime now in charge of New York City and New York State. These officials owe it to the great white race in the State of New York and in the whole United States to protect, safeguard, and preserve in their integrity these principles and ideals so dear to the great white race in America.

The time has come for all true Americans of the Caucasian race to wake up to the dangers that threaten us. There can be no yielding on this great question in order to serve the program and purpose of the Roman-Tammany political machine. We must stand steadfast, and we will stand steadfast, in our purpose and determination to preserve in its integrity race pride and purity and white man's government in the United States. I regret to say that the present disgusting and deplorable situation in New York State, which permitted a white father and mother to be subjected to the humiliating and shameful ordeal of having to submit to the marriage of their daughter to a negro, is not new under the modern Roman-Tammany system in New York City and State. Scores of negroes in Harlem, New York, members of the so-called Democratic Tammany organization, have been permitted to marry white wives with license granted by and with the hearty approval of the State and city government presided over by Governor [Alfred E.] Smith and Jimmy Walker and now by Gov. Franklin Roosevelt and Jimmy Walker. These things are shocking, disgusting, and sickening not only to the Democrats but to the true representatives of the great white race in all parties the country over.

The fact that the Roman Catholic Church[2] permits negroes and whites to belong to the same Catholic Church and to go to the same

---

[2]Senator Heflin was an outspoken anti-Catholic, and frequently made viciously anti-Catholic speeches on the floor of the Senate.

Catholic schools and permits and sanctions the marriage between whites and negroes in the United States is largely responsible for the loose, dangerous, and sickening conditions that exist in New York City and State to-day and the all-important question of preserving the integrity of our race and white supremacy in the United States.

My knowledge of this open and notorious social equality policy, this terrible system in New York State, permitted and approved by Governor Smith, was one of the things that made it impossible for me to support his candidacy for President in 1928. Many States in the Union have laws which forbid marriage between whites and negroes; all of the States should have, and some day will have, such laws. I understand that New York would have had such a law but for the opposition of Governor Smith and his Tammany friends in the legislature. Alabama has such a law, and I helped to put it in the constitution of that State in 1901.

Very truly,

J. Thos. Heflin

[After reading the above letter, Senator Heflin addressed the Senate in part as follows:]

Mr. President, I cry out against [racial intermarriage] in New York, in Alabama, in every State in the Union. I tell you it . . . leads to troublesome things. When negroes in other States read about some negro marrying a white girl up in New York under Tammany rule, it puts the devil in them in other States in the Union. You have a negro buck going out and waylaying a white girl on the way home from school in the rural districts of my State or some other State.

I have in mind now a picture of a beautiful, bright girl in the mountains of north Alabama a few years ago coming home from school, stopping on the road-side in April, the spring of the year, gathering wild flowers, and a negro man leaped out from behind a tree, caught this girl, choked her into unconsciousness, dragged her into the woods, assaulted her, and left her for dead on the roadside. The father of that girl and his neighbors pursued that negro, they caught him, and lynched him, and I approved the act.

Talk to me about being patient, holding your temper, and observing law in a case like that! A father with his heartstrings torn out, with his darling daughter assaulted, disgraced, and almost dead, came up on the black brute who committed the crime. Of course he would kill him, and he ought to have killed him.

That is the way we feel about it. Whenever a negro crosses this dead line between the white and the negro races and lays his black hand on a white woman he deserves to die. That is the way we feel about it, and we are not the only ones who feel that way. The Senator from Idaho [Mr. Borah] once said in this Chamber, "You southerners are not the only ones who lynch negroes for rape. We in the Northern States lynch them just as quickly as you do when they commit that crime against a white woman," and that is true. It is "the call of the blood." . . . .

Changing Attitudes
in the 1930's *

ALLEN J. ELLENDER

To Negroes the progress made by their race between World Wars I and II seemed agonizingly slow and piecemeal. To segregationists it seemed revolutionary, especially in its implications for the future. However haltingly and halfheartedly, the federal government and the national political parties became more and more interested in the race. In 1936, the South lost its stranglehold on the Democratic Party when the party's national convention rescinded the rule requiring a two-thirds vote for nominating presidential candidates. The Supreme Court began to look behind the facade of segregationist claims in applying the separate-but-equal rule, especially in higher education. Groups dedicated to Negro advancement and even to racial integration became bolder and more articulate. The increasing economic strength of middle-class Negroes gave them more security and confidence, and intensified their yearnings for racial equality. All this profoundly affected segregationists. The confidence, even arrogance, they displayed before World War I now gave way to alarm and anguished forebodings about the future. The following address by Senator Allen J. Ellender of Louisiana illustrates these changes, together with the increasing uncertainty of segregationists and their dismay at the course of race relations in the 1930's. Ellender exhibits much of the segregationists' traditional paternalism toward Negroes, but an ambivalence runs through his address. Southern Negroes are "polite by instinct," he says in one instance, but then warns that if given a "foot" they "will attempt to take a yard." Careful reading makes it obvious that he realizes that Negroes are not satisfied with their status in the South. He refuses, however, to admit this or to

*Reprinted from U.S. *Congressional Record,* Vol. 83, Part 1, 75th Cong., 3rd sess. (Washington, D.C.: U.S. Government Printing Office, January 14-20, 1938), pp. 503-04, 571-73, 621, 623, 684-85, 758, 769, 817, 820.

explore its implications for racial policy. He is satisfied to warn of the consequences of equality and integration. The following passages are excerpted from a week-long filibuster Ellender conducted against proposed federal antilynching legislation in 1938.

I believe that the South is well able to take care of this social problem, which problem involves the Negro. The South has had to wrestle with it since the Negro first landed on our shores. We feel that we know the problem, and we believe that the North must be ignorant of the subject, judging by its attitude in the past and its actions at present. . . .

What I fear is that political equality will lead to social equality, and social equality will eventually spell the decay and the downfall of our American civilization. . . . Such decay has followed wherever there has been a mixture of the colored races with the whites. . . .

Mr. President, we understand the Negro. We sympathize with him. A Negro who is born in the South and who has lived there is polite by instinct, but send him up North where he can rub elbows with the whites, where he thinks he is equal to them, and soon he becomes impudent, and if he returns to the South, he gets into trouble. He usually tries to place himself on a social equality with the southern whites and that does not work. . . .

The Negro of the North gets into trouble with the white man of the North when he tries to rub elbows with him—not politically but socially. It is that which the white man of the North resents, and he should. The only white friend the Negro has in the North is the politician and then only when he votes right. As I said a while ago, the Negro from the South is polite by instinct, and he remains in his place and he does not have to be told to do so. He does it by nature. He is taught it from childhood by parents who respect the whites. . . .

[However, the Southern Negro] has not the intelligence to discriminate, and the moment he is given some little authority, a foot of it, he will attempt to take a yard. Up here in Washington it is necessary that I pass through a portion of the Negro district on my way to my apartment every day, and I see many things that are repugnant to a southerner. I will not say this condition would not be permitted in parts of the South, but the white people there know where to draw the line and the associations would not be in the same manner, nor would social equality be permitted or tolerated as it is done here in Washington. We know the colored man to be an imitator, and when he is put on a basis of social equality with the white man he tries to follow and do what the white man does. He may have a certain degree of ambition but his judgment is poor, and when he imagines himself equal to the white man he feels that he can do the same thing with respect to the white race that a white man can, and there is where he gets into trouble. . . .

In those communities in the South where the Negro population is far in excess of the white population Senators will find a greater amount of infraction of the law than in those places where the white population predominates. Why is that? Because in such places the Negroes take for granted that they are stronger and have a right to associate socially with the whites. Then he deserves all the trouble he gets into. I want the Senate to know that at no time in my experience as a lawmaker has the Legislature of Louisiana or any municipal body in Louisiana ever attempted to establish a difference insofar as the property rights and economic rights of the two races are concerned. However, we draw the line with respect to legislation that will make it possible for the white and the colored to rub elbows together; because, I repeat, and I hope it will sink in, political equality leads to social equality, and social equality will eventually spell the decay and downfall of our American civilization.

It may not occur in my lifetime but it is coming. If the attempt is made to amalgamate the two races a Nation of half-breeds will result.

From the action of some northern politicians it seems very obvious that they have agreed to put the Negroes on the same equality with the whites. Their ignorance is pitiful, and I do not think they have considered the result. I do not think the people of the North realize what is being promoted. . . . A small handful of Negroes congregate in large cities in the North, a community here, a community there, and under the leadership of some low white, they are able to get together with the politicians of those states who are willing to trade social-equality legislation for their vote. I cannot believe that the white people of those States know that that is being done. If they did, pride in their own race would prevent it. . . .

America must stand for white supremacy; for if we do not, I say to you that our civilization will deteriorate as did that of Egypt, of India, of Haiti, and of other countries of the world in the past. That is what may happen to us, and I am not willing to silently permit it. . . .

I believe in white supremacy, and as long as I am in the Senate I expect to fight for white supremacy, because I can see, not in my lifetime, perhaps, or in the lifetime of my boy or of his children, but in the years to come, if the amalgamation of whites and Negroes in this country is permitted, that there will be a mongrel race, and there will come to pass the identical condition under which Egypt, India, and other civilizations decayed. . . .

It is my opinion—I may be wrong about it and I hope I am—that ultimately these groups of colored people in the larger cities are going to become stronger and stronger; that they are going to become so powerful that they will be able to hold the balance of power at election time. If ever that happens, then, as surely as I am speaking to you here today, they are going to come to the Congress and demand legislation that will eventually put them on a basis of social equality with the white people of this entire nation. And that is something against which I say we should, by all means, guard. . . .

. . . What I fear is that sooner or later, unless something is done to prevent the amalgamation of the Negro race with the white race, if the Negroes keep on wedging in, getting nearer and nearer to social equality, the white people of this country are bound to see the handwriting on the wall, and I do not know whether there will be any lynchings or not, but there may be a lot of shootings, a lot of bloodshed, race riots as never before. . . .

As far as I am personally concerned, I should not like the idea of deporting the Negroes to Liberia. I believe that we can let them stay here in America, provided they are separated socially and politically from the white people and not permitted to amalgamate with the white race. But, Senators, what I fear, and what the American people should fear, is the continuous encroachment by these little groups of Negroes who come to the Congress and attempt to obtain the passage of bills that will eventually put them on the same plane with the white people—that is what I fear, not only for the Negro but for the white people and for the future of America; and I say that if those agitators succeed, if our Nation shall become so amalgamated that the Congress is presided over by a Negro, or if we have sitting in these seats men of Negro blood, we shall have the same condition existing in this country which existed in the past in Egypt, in India, and other countries. . . .

Mr. President, we in the South have no feeling of hatred against the Negro. We are sympathetic toward him. We understand his problems. We work with him. But what we try to do, what we have always done, and what I hope we always shall do, is to have the colored man keep his place when it comes to the social side of our associations. We do not feel that the Negroes as a race should commingle socially with the white people or marry white people, so that from that union shall come a mongrel race, as happened in Egypt, as happened in India, as has resulted in Haiti, and is happening in Harlem in the city of New York. . . .

. . . If there is an amalgamation of the races, decay of our civilization will surely follow; and amalgamation cannot be stopped, in my mind, if we permit the colored people to keep on encroaching on the whites socially. Political power will bring it about. The Negro may some day become so strong politically that he will be able to command respect for his vote, and he may come to the Senate. Perhaps not next year; perhaps not in the next 50 years; but some day he may come here.

I want to say, however, that the good people of the South, the thinking people, the people as a whole, are very sympathetic with the Negro. We have been considerate of the Negro all of our lives. As a matter of fact, we consider the Negroes our wards. They are a great economic asset to us down South. We treat them kindly; and when I say that, I mean the larger portion of the white race do. I believe, and in fact I know, that the Negro of the South loves the white people of the South; he always has, and in most cases he is obedient to the whites' wishes. . . .

The quicker the Negro people of this Nation can be made to realize that the white man is their superior and that they must work with the white man in order to further advance themselves, I say, the better off will the Negro people be. . . .

As far as I am concerned, I would vote today to repeal the fifteenth amendment, granting suffrage to the Negro before it is too late. I do not want any Negro Senators to sit in the Senate, and I do not want any Negro Governors to sit in the Governor's chair of any State. That is what I mean. I do not want to be misunderstood. I say it charitably, with due respect, with the sympathy that I have and always have had for the Negro people.

The Negro people need the white people more than the white people need the Negro people. History shows that whenever a Negro people has seen the light of civilization it was a light inspired by the white people. The Negroes knew no civilization before they came to

Egypt. They came uncivilized from dark Africa. When they came to India they knew no civilization. They knew nothing beside the barbarism under which they had lived in dark Africa.

The Negroes came to this country, to America, in bondage. They came here as slaves, and they did not know the light of civilization until they reached the shores of America. I say that the American people have been a blessing to the Negroes. The Negroes have prospered here, they have progressed. But the Lord pity them, and the Lord pity us, if there is an amalgamation of the Negroes with the whites. . . .

If the colored man is given a foot by way of political equality, he is going to demand a yard, and if he is given a yard, he will demand a rod, and if he is given a rod, he will demand 5 miles.

World War II: Increasing Racial Tensions*

THEODORE G. BILBO

World War II, like World War I, was accompanied by increasing racial tensions. To an even greater extent than their fathers in the earlier holocaust, Negroes in World War II were conscious of the fact that the democratic rhetoric of wartime America bore little relationship to the actualities of segregation and discrimination. Moreover, the war effort was much more massive than that of 1917-18, and caused severe strains in the traditional relations between whites and Negroes. Tested in the crucible of a total war against tyranny and dictatorship, Jim Crowism was found wanting. The most serious race riot in American history between Reconstruction and 1965 occurred in Detroit in 1943, and tensions mounted in other areas. Negroes became more insistent in demanding better treatment as the price of their support for the war effort. President Roosevelt was more sympathetic than Woodrow Wilson had been, and the federal government attempted to curtail some of the more glaring instances of discrimination, especially in federal employment. The reaction of Southern segregationists to these developments is mirrored in the following address by Mississippi's Senator Theodore G. Bilbo, one of the most outspoken demagogues and race baiters in the South's history. The address, delivered on March 22, 1944 to a joint session of the Mississippi legislature, illustrates the persistence of traditional segregationist views in the South. Bilbo's racial ideas are summarized in his work, Take Your Choice: Separation or Mongrelization, *which he published in 1947.*

---

*Reprinted from U.S. *Congressional Record,* Vol. XC, Part 9, 78th Cong., 2d sess. (Washington, D.C.: Government Printing Office, 1944), pp. A1795-A1802.

In addition to putting forth a total effort to hasten the winning of the war, 1944 presents another challenge to the American people; that is, the preservation of our dual system of constitutional government. We all realize and understand that in time of war, our Federal Government must exercise extraordinary powers and we are in full accord with the belief that our Federal Government should do everything that is necessary to protect the life of this Nation and to win the war in which we are engaged. However, our democracy must not be destroyed in the name of war. . . .

It is not my purpose here today to tell you of all the possible threats to our dual system of constitutional government. . . . Being States' rights Democrats, you are already aware of Washington's growing power, you know that the destruction of the rights of the 48 States and the wiping out of States' lines would open the flood gates and prepare the way for the ultimate destruction of freedom, made safe by our dual system of Government.

[We Southerners] have implicit faith in the American people and are confident that the people of this Nation will face openly and squarely any threat which may come to our democracy. . . . However, there is one bill now pending before the United States Senate directly affecting States' rights which I want to discuss briefly with you. That bill . . . is the so-called anti-poll-tax bill and I want to bring this bill with all its implications before you, together with a full discussion of the great race problem which we are now forced to openly consider.

The anti-poll-tax bill, which would make unlawful by Federal statute, the requirement for the payment of a poll tax as a prerequisite to voting in a primary or other election for national officers, is clearly unconstitutional. . . .

Nowhere in the Constitution is Congress given the power to strike down or add to the qualifications for electors as set up by the sovereign States nor is the Congress given the power to define the qualifications or prerequisites for electors. The decisions of the United States Supreme Court are unanimous in holding that the poll-tax laws are constitutional and nondiscriminatory. The tax applies equally to whites and Negroes and the proceeds are generally used for educational purposes.

Regardless of what any of us may think of the poll tax as such and regardless of whether or not we are in favor of its abolition by our State—just here let me say that for the holding of our white party primaries I have long contended that the poll tax should be abolished—nevertheless, the Congress has no power under the Federal Constitution to pass this bill outlawing the tax. . . .

If the Congress succeeds in abolishing the poll tax, then the precedent will be set for the abolition by the Congress of any or all of our franchise laws[,] and our ballots in Mississippi, and in all the other 47 States, will be at the mercy of the Federal Government. Constitutional government, as we have known it for over 150 years, would then no longer exist and the rights of the sovereign States would be destroyed.

In the face of these facts, you may rightly ask: Who are the advocates of this infamous unconstitutional bill? Why are the forces behind this piece of legislation so strong? . . .

There are various individuals and organizations sponsoring this bill, but the main pressure groups behind it are Negro organizations. They are able to wield this power because the Negro vote in some nine northern States constitutes something of a balance-of-power between the white Democratic and Republican Parties. And these groups are determined to make an all-out effort to secure passage of this anti-poll-tax bill because the enactment of this piece of legislation is one of the steps—the entering wedge—toward the fulfillment of the "full equality" program which the Negro leaders have launched in this time of war. . . .

Thus, the poll-tax bill brings the entire race question before the American people. . . .

Of course during the days of slavery, the relations between the white race and the Negro race were definitely fixed, but with the freeing of the slaves, immediately the question of the status of the newly freed Negroes became a national issue. . . .

[During the days of Radical Reconstruction traditional racial patterns were disrupted, but the Radicals and carpetbaggers were soon driven from the South.] And as white supremacy was restored . . . the relations between the races began [once more] to take on a definite fixed pattern. With some 4,000,000 ignorant, freed slaves in their midst, the southern people put into operation the policy of segregation of the races.

With separate facilities and separate accommodations for the white people and for the Negroes, the color line was drawn in every walk of life below Mason and Dixon's line. Accepted by the members of both races just as they accepted the air they breathed, the policy of segregation has remained in the Southland, and the attacks which, down through the years have been made on it from the outside have met with complete failure. However, it has become necessary for us to consider and to openly discuss the forces which are today attempting to destroy the color line.

The so-called leaders of the Negro race have deliberately chosen this time of war to launch their program of full equality of the races in this country. The March-on-Washington movement, a Negro group headed by A. Philip Randolph, president of the Brotherhood of Sleeping Car Porters, carried their demands to the White House in June 1941. Thousands of Negroes threatened to march in mass upon Washington in what they termed "protest of discrimination in Government employment and in the war industries." After conferences with the Negro leaders, President Roosevelt issued Executive Order 8802 and the march on Washington was called off. This order, issued June 25, 1941, provided that:

There shall be no discrimination in the employment of workers in defense industries or Government because of race, creed, color, or national origin.

The order also established the Committee on Fair Employment Practices to carry this policy into effect. There is nothing in Executive Order 8802 about abolishing segregation and ordering the mixing of the races. However, as a result of the order there is today no segregation in the United States Government offices in Washington.

In the Federal offices in Washington, whites and Negroes work in the same rooms, the same offices, eat together at the same cafeterias, use the same rest rooms and recreational facilities. White girls may be assigned as secretaries to Negro men, and Negro girls may be sent to the offices of white officials. . . . In many bureaus and departments, the mixing of the races has gone so far that southern girls going to the capital city to work, have returned to their homes. Others, who for various reasons must remain there to work, find such conditions almost unbearable. . . .

The March-on-Washington group proposes to abolish segregation completely throughout the United States and to bring about the full political, economic, and social equality of the races. So that you will have no doubts about their demands, I wish to read you excerpts from an article, "Why Should We March," by A. Philip Randolph, head of the movement, appearing in the November 1942 Survey Graphic:

... What are the reasons for this state of mind? The answer is: discrimination, segregation, Jim Crow. ...

It is to meet this situation squarely with direct action that the March-on-Washington movement launched its present program of protest mass meetings.... Meetings of such magnitude were unprecedented among Negroes. ...

The March-on-Washington movement is essentially a movement of the people. . . . The plan of a protest march has not been abandoned. Its purpose would be to demonstrate that American Negroes are in deadly earnest, and all out for their full rights. No power on earth can cause them today to abandon their fight to wipe out every vestige of second-class citizenship and the dual standards that plague them. ...

By fighting for their rights now, American Negroes are helping to make America a moral and spiritual arsenal of democracy. Their fight against the poll tax, against lynch law, segregation, and Jim Crow, their fight for economic, political, and social equality, thus becomes part of the global war for freedom.

This is the kind of propaganda being fed to the Negro masses. It is the contention of these Negro leaders that segregation is in itself discrimination. This question has been before the United States Supreme Court on a number of occasions and the Court has held that segregation is not discrimination as long as adequate accommodations are provided for both races. . . .

At this same mass meeting there was also a speech made by Roy Wilkins, assistant secretary of the National Association for the Advancement of Colored People. This association is another of the Negro organizations leading in this fight for full equality of the races. Wilkins declared:

We refuse to listen to the weak-kneed of both races who tell us not to raise controversies during the war. We believe, on the contrary, that we are doing a patriotic duty in raising them.

I am sorry to say that certain religious leaders of the Negro race are joining the organizations and groups already named in spreading the preachings of social equality to the Negro masses. The following article was clipped from the New York Herald Tribune and will show you how far some of these Negro preachers are going:

The Reverend James H. Robinson, pastor of the Negro Presbyterian Church of the Master, 86 Morningside Avenue, in an address yesterday in Milbank Chapel, Teachers College, Columbia University, described the race problem in the United States as "very bad" and suggested that the time might come when certain groups would protest by forceful means.

Speaking at a 3-day conference on religion in the modern world, sponsored by Columbia University, Mr. Robinson asserted that Negro soldiers who had been taught to kill those standing in the way of democracy "are not going to discriminate between a German and an American who does the same thing." He warned the 75 delegates that if Americans did not approach the racial problem with frankness and courage, they might see a march on Washington, or race riots, after the war.

He said the morale of Negro troops is "very low" because they are being discriminated against by other soldiers in the Army. Similar discrimination, he asserted, exists in war plants, and is lowering morale among Negroes there.

"The Negro soldier," he said "hears platitudes of democracy, but can see no adequate demonstration of them. It is lamentable, but true, that Negro soldiers believe the outcome of the war will be determined by how strongly the Russians come."

. . . I am sure you have read in the Jackson [Mississippi] Daily News of Wednesday, March 8, the Washington story of Dr. Studebaker and his Negro assistant, Dr. Ambrose Caliver, calling on the colleges and universities of the South to open wide their doors for the matriculation of Negro students. . . . [The Daily News] editorial on this report from the Office of Education out of Washington, under the title of "Go Straight to Hell," meets with my full and complete endorsement. [The editor] is right when he says that the South won't do it and that not in this generation and never in the future while Anglo-Saxon blood flows in our veins will the people of the South open the doors of their colleges and universities for Negro students. I repeat that [the editor] is right. We will tell our Negro-loving Yankee friends to go straight to hell.

Another group of Negroes recently sounded the warning that they would use force if necessary to win the full equality that they are seeking. This group visited me in my office in Washington shortly after I became chairman of the Senate Committee on the District of Columbia. Practically every Negro organization in Washington had a representative in the group, and they wanted me to know the demands which they were making for full political, economic, and social equality. When I expressed my doubts as to their receiving what they were asking, one spokesman said that if that were true, then Negroes had just as well quit buying War bonds and get out of the war effort. It was further said by one member of the group that Negroes intended to secure full equality and would do so by force, if necessary, when the war is over. There you have their demands in no uncertain terms. . . .

In February the C.I.O. opened a canteen in Washington for service men and women. . . . On opening night there were some 200 service men and women present. There were about an equal number of white and Negro soldiers who attended and white girls and Negro girls served as hostesses to those soldiers in equal numbers. Can you picture such social affairs taking place in our Nation's Capital? In speaking of the opening of the canteen, Congressman McKenzie, of Louisiana, asked:

How can anyone be a party to encouraging white girls into the arms of Negro soldiers at a canteen while singing Let Me Call You Sweetheart?

. . . Have we reached the place in this country when we are going to permit our white girls to attend social functions with Negro soldiers? If we do permit such, can we profess to be surprised at what the results may be? . . . Are our soldiers and sailors fighting to save this Nation, or are they fighting so that we may become a mongrelized people? Practicing social equality of the races is certainly the surest way to destroy the culture of the white race. . . .

We in the Southland, being fully aware of the attempts to break down segregation and implant social equality of the races throughout the Nation are ready to do some plain talking. The Negro leaders have brought this issue of race relations before us in this time of war; they have stated their demands so we have no alternative but to tell them where we stand.

We in Mississippi are justly proud of the harmonious relations existing here among the races. Our population is almost equally divided and we are glad to have peaceful, law-abiding Negroes within our midst. We ask no Negro to leave our State; at the same time we ask no discontented Negro to remain.

Three-fourths of the Nation's 12,800,000 Negroes are living and earning a livelihood in the South. We have an established policy of segregation known and understood by the members of both races. We recognize the right of a Negro to hire Negroes in preference to white people and the white employer has the same right. The right of Southern white people to operate political associations and hold their primaries, excluding Negroes, is no more to be questioned than the right of Negroes to form political or social clubs, excluding white people. Certainly Negroes may own and conduct their own restaurants, hotels and shops exclusively for themselves, just as white people may do likewise. The races shall have equal and separate accommodations on busses and trains; and separate public schools shall be maintained. Equal and exact justice shall be accorded both races under the law, but segregation of the races shall be enforced. Honest and intelligent Southern white and colored people agree with this policy. In commenting on the recent Detroit race riots, a Negro leader in Arkansas, Rev. Thomas J. Brown, editor of the Eastern Arkansas World, made the following statement:

> The only way to live peaceably and unmolested in the South, North, East, and West is for every kind to [live to] himself; whether it be race, clan or tribe. Henry W. Longfellow wrote, "Birds of a feather flock together." . . .
>
> The average Negro is proud of his race and its achievement and would not care to undermine its solidarity by amalgamation or intermarriage with other races;
>
> No one needs to be uneasy about the Negro in the South wanting to associate with white folks. He does not even want to live in the same block with them. He does not care to even sit in his front room or eat with him at his table. We don't want to ride with him. We are contented to reside in a Negro section of our towns, go to our own church which is pastored by a black man; send our children to school where they can be under the loving care of Negro teachers.[1] . . .

The Negro race in the South is fortunate to have such a leader as Reverend Brown, and I think he would agree with me that it is difficult, if not impossible, to understand why any group or individual outside the Southland would want to destroy the harmonious race relations which exist here. . . . The three reasons for the destruction of all racial barriers throughout the Nation are stated by the Militant Church Movement [of] Louisville, Ky., in the following manner:

> The Militant Church Movement affirms:
>
> That color does not affect anything but the outer surface of the skin. . . .
>
> That every act of racial hatred or discrimination is in violation of the will of

---

[1]The sentiments of the Rev. Mr. Brown were of course labeled "Uncle Tomism" by more militant Negroes in the 1940's. The similarity between his views and some of those expressed by some militant Negro nationalists today is therefore both ironic and striking.

the founders of this Republic and the principles of Christianity upon which this Nation was built. Thomas Jefferson, who wrote the Declaration of Independence, freed his slaves to prove his sincerity in declaring that all men are born free and equal.

That no church is Christian that is not built on the foundation laid down by its founder, Jesus Christ, namely, the fatherhood of God, the brotherhood of man, and the Golden Rule. . . .

Now, I propose to show the falsity of all three of these reasons. First, history and science both defy the statement that "color does not affect anything but the outer surface of the skin." Historical and scientific research has established three propositions beyond all controversy:

First, The white race has founded, developed, and maintained every civilization known to the human race.[2]

Second, The white race, having founded, developed, and maintained a civilization, has never been known, in all history, to lose that civilization as long as the race was kept white.

Third, The white man has never kept unimpaired the civilization he has founded and developed after his blood stream has been adulterated by the blood stream of another race, more especially another race so widely diverse in all its inherent qualities as the black race. . . .

The superior ability of the Caucasian man is evidenced by his endless creation of art, science, law, religion, literature, and every other form of activity known to man down through the ages. Against these achievements, what has the African to offer? What history? What art? What science? What morality? And who will deny the almightiness of heredity? Let the blood stream be corrupted and nothing can ever restore its purity. If you do not accept this as true, then you brand as false both history and biology. . . .

In the second place, this group has tried to justify full equality of the races in this country in the name of democracy, the name of the founding fathers, and the teaching of Thomas Jefferson. I quote Jefferson's own words:

Nothing is more certainly written in the book of fate, than that these people are to be free; nor is it less certain that the two races, equally free, cannot live in the same government. Nature, habit, opinion have drawn indelible lines of distinction between them. . . .

---

[2]This of course credits Caucasians not only for the civilizations of Egypt, the ancient Near East, Greece, and Rome, but also those of India, China, Japan, Mexico (the Aztecs), and Peru (the Incas). In his post-war work, *Take Your Choice: Separation or Mongrelization,* Bilbo specifically asserted these claims.

The founders of this Republic never dreamed of it being anything but a white nation. We owe an immeasurable debt to our forefathers who preserved us white through 300 years of race contact. . . .

The third argument used by the Militant Church group, that of religion, to break down all racial barriers has been frequently used. It was used at one time by the British missionaries in South Africa, and we have before us the practical results of their teachings that all races are of one blood. The mix-breeds of the Cape of Good Hope are evidence of the influence of these ignorant, Negro-loving missionaries who brought disaster along with their teachings. The doctrines of the missionaries were soon changed and they ceased to teach social equality, but who could undo the damage which they had done? The present missionary teaches of the same God and the same Christ and tells the same story of redemption, but one social teaching has been changed. . . .

History clearly shows that the white race is the custodian of the gospel of Jesus Christ and that the white man is entrusted with the spreading of that gospel.

The gospel, of course, is universal; it is missionary in scope; and it is given to all men of all nations. Yet what can be more foreign to the ideals of the Christian religion than amalgamation and miscegenation? Anyone who would, in the name of Christianity, make us a negroid people betrays his religion and his race.

It should be the desire of both races to maintain racial integrity and have their blood remain pure. If religion teaches the destruction of the races and commits the error of preaching the mixture of all bloods, then what can the missionaries and ministers do to give to the unborn generations the racial heritage which is rightfully theirs? A. H. Shannon, author of Racial Integrity, poses this question: "Which is better, a mongrel race, whose origin is in sin, and which represents the worst of all races; or a race, whatever its limitations, yet true to its own racial peculiarities and striving to attain, intact, the best and highest of which it is capable? . . . "

Those who would teach us social equality of the races remind us of the fatherhood of God and the brotherhood of man. Why place a fallacious interpretation on these two phrases? If we are to spiritualize "Fatherhood of God," then why must we literalize "Brotherhood of man"? Both the fatherhood of God and the brotherhood of man are spiritual, and anyone who would interpret the brotherhood of man in such a manner as to destroy the blood of the white race would destroy the race which has through the centuries proven itself to be the custodian of the gospel of Christ, of his spiritual and ethical teachings. . . .

One of the most pregnant sources of corrupting the minds of our people on the race question is the apostasy of ministers and preachers of practically every denomination expounding the theories of the Christian religion under the favorite texts of Brotherhood of Mankind, Fatherhood of God, and All of One Blood. Some of these negrophilistic preachers with their false interpretations of the real teachings of the Christian religion, pouring out a lot of maudlin sentiment and ecclesiastical rot, tend to make their followers, here in the South and in the North, believe that, under God, the white man is no better than the Negro and that, if you want to go to Heaven, you had better take the sons and daughters of Ethiopia into your fond embraces. . . .

Any preacher or minister who would take advantage of his divine calling to thus destroy the integrity of his race and contaminate and corrupt the blood of his fathers should by his own church be unfrocked and never permitted to smack his traitorous lips on another yellow-legged chicken. . . .

There are those who would tear away [the] racial pride [of Southern whites], knowing full well that it would plunge the Southland into hopeless depths of hybridization. Implant the doctrines of social equality below the Mason-Dixon line, and the result will be a mongrelized Southland. And if the transmitted germ plasma is destroyed, nothing shall ever restore it; neither wealth, nor culture, nor science, nor art, nor morality, nor religion itself.

To southerners this is not a question of individual morality or of self-respect or of individual accomplishments. Every child that is born is born not only of its immediate parents but of all its ancestry. Every child is a child of its race, and heredity plays its part upon it and upon all its descendants. However weak the white man, behind him stands Europe; however strong the black, behind him lies Africa. . . .

We people of the South must draw the color line tighter and tighter, and any white man or woman who dares to cross that color line should be promptly and forever ostracized. No compromise on this great question should be tolerated, no matter who the guilty parties are, whether in the church, in public office, or in the private walks of life. Ostracize them if they cross the color line and treat them as a Negro or as his equal should be treated. . . .

It is imperative that we face squarely and frankly the conditions which confront us. We must not sit idly by, but we must ever be on guard to protect the southern ideals, customs, and traditions that we love and believe in so firmly and completely. There are some issues that we may differ upon, but on racial integrity, white supremacy, and love of the Southland we will stand together until we pass on to another world.

In Defense of
School Segregation*

White Intervenors in Stell v. Savannah-Chatham
County Board of Education

The efforts of southern whites to prevent public school integration in recent years have been many and varied. One of the strangest has been their effort to reverse the Supreme Court decision in Brown v. Board of Education of Topeka (1954), in which the Court set aside the separate-but-equal precedent and destroyed the constitutional basis for public school segregation. In a footnote to that decision, the Court cited works by several social scientists, labeling them "modern authority" for its statement that racial segregation in public schools is psychologically damaging to Negro children. Unable to overturn the Brown ruling on legal or constitutional grounds some segregationists decided in the early 1960's to challenge it on social science grounds. The most significant of their challenges was Stell v. Savannah-Chatham County Board of Education. The Stell case was originally brought by Negroes in an effort to integrate the public schools of Savannah, Georgia, under the precedent of the Brown decision. A group of white parents petitioned to enter the case in order to challenge the Brown decision (the legal basis of the Negroes' suit) on grounds that (1) the social science incorporated in the decision was scientifically invalid, and (2) "the bulk of available scientific evidence and modern authority in 1963 support the view that race is a valid unit of classification for educational purposes." The following are excerpts from their petition to enter the case and the

---

*Reprinted from Record on Appeal from the U.S. District Court for the Southern District of Georgia—Savannah Division—To the U.S. Court of Appeals for the Fifth Circuit, Stell v. Savannah-Chatham County Board of Education, Civil Action no. 1316, Pleas and Answer to Intervenors, 4-13; and *ibid.,* Brief and Argument in support of Motion to Intervene, 17-19.

accompanying Brief and Argument. (Note: The Stell *case came to naught; the Fifth Circuit Court of Appeals refused to hear it.)*

Existing ethnic group differences in educational achievement and psychometric intelligence are of such a magnitude that extensive racial integration will seriously impair the academic standards and educational opportunities for the petitioners and other White children of Savannah-Chatham County. The mean mental age of White school children in Savannah-Chatham County ranges from two to four school years ahead of the mean mental age of Negro school children in Savannah-Chatham County. If the Negro and White children are educated in the same schools and in the same rooms with the same teachers and all are grouped on the basis of academic achievement the White students will average from two to four years younger in chronological age than the Negro students. On the other hand if such children are grouped on the basis of chronological age, existing academic standards in the now all-White schools cannot be maintained and the system of education for the White children will be virtually destroyed, without any corresponding benefit to the academic progress of the Negro students.

. . . Existing ethnic group differences in socio-moral and behavioral standards in Savannah and Chatham County are of such a magnitude that extensive racial integration will seriously impair prevailing socio-moral standards in the now all-White schools. . . . The rates of emotional instability, behavioral delinquency, illegitimacy and venereal diseases among Negro children and their parents are vastly greater than among White children and their parents. Since all children bring the influences of the home with them to school, the enforced integration of petitioners and those they represent with said Negro students will, of necessity, result in the impairment of the cultural and educational opportunities of the White children. . . . Said ethnic group differences exist now and will continue to exist for the term of the petitioners' presence in the public schools of Savannah-Chatham County, and if this Honorable Court does not by its orders and decrees, protect the petitioning school children and the class they represent there is no way whereby they may be protected against such baneful influences all of which will affect their minds and hearts in a way unlikely ever to be undone.

. . . The following significant psychometric test differences exist between Negro school children and White school children throughout the nation and to a similar or greater extent in Savannah-Chatham County:

(1) The intelligence quotients of Negro children are 15 to 20 points, on the average, below those of Whites.

(2) Negro overlap of the median White intelligence quotient ranges from 2 to 25 per cent (equality would require 50 per cent).

(3) Approximately 6 times as many Whites as Negroes fall in the "gifted child" category (I.Q. greater than 139).

(4) Approximately 6 times as many Negroes as Whites fall below 70 I.Q.—that is, in the "feeble-minded" group.

(5) Negro-White differences in mean test score occur in all types of mental tests, but the Negro lag is greatest in tests of an abstract nature, such as problems involving reasoning, deduction and comprehension. These are the functions called for in education above the lowest levels.

(6) Differences between Negro and White children increase with chronological age, the gap in performance being largest at the high school and college levels.

(7) Large and significant differences in favor of Whites appear when socioeconomic factors have been equated.

(8) In general the greater the admixture of White genes the closer does the Negro approach the White performance level both in school and afterwards.

. . . These ethnic differences exist regardless of whether or not there is legal or institutionalized segregation. Racial segregation is not a cause but is a natural and rational consequence of such differences and disparities. . . .

. . . Racial differences in physical, mental, psychical, and behavioral traits between plaintiffs and petitioners are, to a large extent, genetically determined and are a natural result of the biological processes of race formation. . . . The origin and formation of the various races of mankind have resulted from differential and adaptive selection of hereditary variations (arising from mutations and genetic drift), in reproductively isolated populations. These differences have then been perpetuated and stabilized through continued isolation and inbreeding of the major races over long periods of time. . . . Diagnostic anatomical, psychological, and bio-chemical traits characterize the major races of man. There are significant differences in cerebral morphology and physical constitution which are structurally related to racial differences in mental, psychical and behavioral traits. Said differences constitute a rational basis for segregation of races in schools, particularly among the young and immature.

. . . The operation of a bi-racial school system in Savannah-Chatham County is rational and is a reasonable classification, based upon the teachings of modern social science with respect to the role of race and physically observable racial differences in group dynamics.

Modern social science, in the field of race relations, teaches:

(a) That selective associational or racial preference is a universal human trait, which manifests itself in a variety of cultures and at a very early age—even in pre-school children—and may have a genetic basis, arising out of the biological processes of race formation;

(b) That physically observable racial differences form the basis of preferential association or social distance—i.e., the disposition of one group to avoid intimate social contact with another—and thus act as a focal point for group orientation.

(c) That the association of young persons with members of their own racial or ethnic group is beneficial and indeed necessary for their optimal personality development and social maturity. Ethnic group integrity (i.e., the association of individuals with those whom they share a common biological origin, cultural heritage, and conscious-ness of kind) aids in the development of a more stable self-concept, fulfills in-group identity needs, and provides an atmosphere most conducive to optimum social growth and maturity. . . . To compel them to associate with members of a markedly diverse racial group while in attendance at the public schools of Chatham County would impair their personality development at a critical period in their social growth.

. . . The compulsory association of the two diverse and physically distinct racial groups in the public schools of Savannah-Chatham County will lead to an increase in tension and promote social dishar-mony due to the physical and temperamental contrasts between the two racial groups and due to the universal tendency of individuals to associate along racial lines where the diversity is gross.

. . . Where a program of extensive racial integration introduces a large proportion of Negroes into previously all-White schools, the above mentioned mental, physical, moral and emotional differences between the White children and Negro children causes [sic]:

(a) Serious sex problems due to the lower moral standards of the Negroes and the placement in the same classrooms of more mature

Negroes who are two to four years older than the more academically advanced White children.

(b) A severe increase in disciplinary problems resulting from the more prevalent use of violence, vile profanity, lascivious sexual behavior, thefts, vandalism, cheating, lying, and other anti-social conduct on the part of the Negro students.

(c) A severe drain on the time and talents of the teachers of Savannah-Chatham County due to their increased preoccupation with disciplinary problems. . . . Neither the White nor the Colored school teachers of Savannah-Chatham County are equipped by training and physical strength to cope with the disciplinary problems that unavoidably result from enforced associations of said dissimilar ethnic groups.

. . . Where racial integration introduces a large proportion of Negroes into previously all White schools the decline in academic and socio-moral standards and the increase in social tension and interracial friction adversely affects the educational opportunities for the White children and results in the withdrawal from the public schools of those White children who are able to afford other schooling. Petitioners and their parents are unable to afford private schools and lack the means to run away as have those employed by the Government in Washington, D.C. or those who enjoy great wealth, high income, or political power. Unless this Court protects the right of petitioners to enjoy adequate and decent educational facilities and the right to selectively associate with those children with whom they share a common biological origin, cultural heritage, and consciousness of kind, the petitioners will be denied those basic rights which the children of the economically and politically privileged possess.

. . . Even in hypocritically so-called "well-integrated" situations (i.e., where the proportion of Negroes is minimal, where there is no historical heritage or tradition of legal segregation, and where there is no overt racial animosity) social preferences in heterogeneous groups occur along racial lines. Irrespective of cause, free social contact between the two races represented by plaintiffs on the one hand and petitioners on the other will create special social problems that immature school children are not equipped to handle in the prevailing social climate such as: interracial social intercourse, interracial dating, interracial dancing, etc. Should the Savannah-Chatham County School Board restrict or eliminate such school social activities, petitioners would be deprived of the opportunity afforded by those social relationships which are necessary for the development of a healthy and mature personality. Thus, should granting relief requested in plaintiffs' complaint result in the compulsory integration of such a limited number of Negroes into public schools of Chatham County, Georgia, as is hypocritically described as "well-integrated", and the educational and socio-moral standards were not so seriously impaired, as they would be in the event of full integration, exacerbated social problems would nevertheless arise and would in general tend to deprive petitioners of many of the benefits they now receive in a bi-racial school system.

. . . If Negro children suffer personality impairments, such impairments (i.e., self-devaluation and identification with Caucasian values and standards of beauty) are not the consequence of legally sanctioned racial segregation *per se,* but rather of the total social situation. The "ideal of beauty" of a particular society or culture is an idealization of the physical features of the dominant racial type, and individuals and groups whose physical appearance manifestly diverge from the dominant standards are faced with serious problems of psychological adjustment. Since the American Negro resides in a culture complex where Caucasian or Europoid esthetic values and preferences prevail and will continue to prevail in the immediate future, the psycho-behavioral syndrome evinced by Negroes results from their status as a physically distinct minority group and not as a result of legally sanctioned school segregation.

. . . Negroes attending racially separate schools where they are socialized in their own group tend: (a) to have more substantial self-concepts and a lesser rejection of their own race; (b) to suffer less frustration and repressed hostility; and (c) to exhibit greater race pride and solidarity.

Racial integration of the schools of Chatham County will, (a) intensify personality tensions and psychodynamic difficulties of Negro children instead of alleviating them; and (b) cause adverse psychological effects in the Negro children from being forced to compete with academically more advanced White children, and on the contrary will not serve any beneficial purpose for any of the school children who are parties in this cause.

. . . The establishment and the maintenance of separate but equal educational facilities for Whites and Negroes in Savannah-Chatham County, is the only means dictated by the reason and experience of those affected, for affording to both Negro children and White children equal protection of the laws, and the only means whereby the members of each race may develop the unique combination of different abilities and traits each has so that the radically diverse talents, traits, gifts and capacities of each child and each race may be developed to the fullest extent for the benefit of all.

. . . Racial differences are factual differences[.] . . . Neither [petitioners] nor those represented by them in Savannah-Chatham County have ever been a party or parties to or represented by counsel in any cause wherein an integration decree was entered and hence . . . they are not bound by any decrees heretofore rendered between other parties. Furthermore, . . . in no case where integration of races has been ordered in public schools, has the court's decree been based upon experience or the lawful evidence of impartial ethnologists, geneticists, anthropologists, psychologists or sociologists, and in consequence, the integration decrees heretofore rendered have been based upon records wherein there was no evidence of such facts as are alleged in this intervention. . . . Had the evidence of experienced citizens and impartial scientists been developed before the courts on such pleadings as would have authorized the same, the courts would necessarily have found that there are such vast differences between the two ethnic groups, as are alleged in this intervention. . . . Such rational findings of facts would have resulted in decrees holding that racial segregation of school children affords the children of each group the fullest opportunity for development, beneficially affecting their motivation to learn[.] . . . Racial integration has a tendency to retard the educational and mental development of Negroes and Whites and deprives them of the many benefits they naturally receive in competitive association with those of their own kin, kind and level. . . .

. . . .

In summary, the bulk of available scientific evidence and modern authority in 1963 support the view that race is a valid unit of classification for educational purposes and that the operation of separate schools on the basis of race and color is a reasonable decision. Racial differences between Whites and Negroes have been demonstrated in psychometric intelligence and educational achievement, temperament, emotional instability, behavioral delinquency, illegitimacy and venereal disease, as well as in the neuro-anatomical basis of these intellectual and behavioral characteristics. All of these traits are directly related to school performance and affect the quality of the educational facilities since each child is directly affected by those other children with whom he is compelled to associate.

The evidence from social science research on the role of race and physically observable racial differences in group identification demonstrates that even if skin color were the only difference between Whites and Negroes, this would be a valid and rational basis for establishing separate schools, and the best method of enabling the members of each racial group to develop their own unique combination of abilities to the fullest.

Since there is individual variability and some overlapping between the two racial groups for each *single* trait, it has sometimes been argued that this should result in separation by ability groups (all those above 100 IQ, for example, being assigned to one school, and all those below 100 IQ being assigned to another school) and not by race. This would be reasonable if the *only* difference between the two ethnic groups were an overlapping statistical distribution of a *single* trait subject to precise measurement—such as IQ scores—and if the role of observable physical differences in social processes were ignored.

However, it should be emphasized that the White and Negro races differ in numerous psychological and behavioral traits—some of which are subject to precise measurement (such as intelligence test performance), and some of which can be described only in qualitative terms (such as personality traits). It is the *totality* of such differences, not any *one single* difference, that must be carefully considered in any evaluation of school segregation by parents and school officials. This is the same principle of frequency probabilities which underlies insurance rate classifications. . . . On the same basis, race is the most convenient and rational classification for the operation of separate schools, since the race, not the individual, is the unit of inheritance and evolutionary change. The White and Negro races have, on the one hand, different biological origins derived from their separate evolutionary development. On the other hand, the two racial groups live under separate and diverse socio-economic circumstances. Both of these factors are beyond the power of the school board or the parent to influence—whether by racial integration of schools or any other action.

Political and Constitutional
Views of
Segregationists Today

WILLIAM J. SIMMONS and RICHARD D. MORPHEW

*Racial issues have dominated Southern politics (and sometimes na-
tional politics, too) throughout the 20th century. In the South, white
supremacists made politics, as well as state and local governments,
into instruments for preserving their racial policies and keeping the
Negro in his "place." On the national level, they used their power
and influence to accomplish the same ends, chiefly by minimizing
federal "interference" in southern race policy. Politics, in short, was
the segregationists' first line of defense.*

*The political thought of segregationists, like the politics of segre-
gation, was alternately opportunistic, radical, and reactionary. In the
last generation, actions by the federal government, including the
Supreme Court, on behalf of Negroes and integration have caused
segregationists much political difficulty, and have incidentally demonstrated the limitations of their political ideas. The following addresses
by two officials of the Citizens' Councils of America (headquarters:
Jackson, Mississippi) summarize the political and constitutional views
of segregationists today. The first excerpt is from the address by
William J. Simmons, administrator of the Citizens' Councils, delivered to the organizational meeting of the Greater Los Angeles
Citizens' Council, June 30, 1964. The second is from an address by
Richard D. Morphew, managing editor of* The Citizen, *official journal
of the Councils, to students of the California Institute of Technology,
Pasadena, California, October 17, 1962.*

[William J. Simmons]

There is no need for me to remind you of the importance of this meeting. I am sure all of you are well aware that something is terribly wrong with our society, and you are here in this room tonight because you want to do something about it. There is a long way to go, and much to be done, of course, but a beginning has to be made. Everyone knows the first step is the hardest; there is no better time to take it than right now.

Let us agree in the beginning what we are concerned about and why we meet. To put it simply, we believe that an all-powerful Federal government is taking us down the road to tyranny, with the resulting loss of our personal freedoms. No one will argue that we are well on the way. We also believe in social separation of the white and negro [sic] races. Certainly no one will contend that we are not threatened in that respect. We know that these two cornerstones—liberty and racial integrity or social separation of the races—provide the foundation upon which our system of social, political and economic values is built. And we know that they are being attacked simultaneously.

The reason is not hard to find. It lies in the wave of equalitarianism which started in our educational system, especially in teachers' colleges like Columbia, before World War I. An early leader was Dr. John Dewey, father of progressive education, who was also a charter member of the NAACP. The equalitarian movement spread slowly from such teaching centers until the shock of the great depression and the advent of the New Deal provided a fertile ground for its proliferation.

It would hardly be too much to say that dating from the nineteen-thirties the nation has been managed from Harvard, with occasional ideological assists from Columbia. The process started with men like Felix Frankfurter, who incidentally was chairman of the NAACP legal committee and won its first Supreme Court case in 1915. As a member of the New Deal brain trust, he filled the expanding ranks of bureaucrats in Franklin Roosevelt's time with proteges from Harvard who had been trained in Fabian socialism under the cloak of planned economy. The process continues to this day. In fact, one may judge the degree of leftward drift by recalling that even Felix Frankfurter eventually came to be regarded as one of the more "conservative" members of the United States Supreme Court.

The line of attack initiated by the equalitarian socialists who now control our government has taken three principal routes.

First, was the objective of reaching a concordat with the great socialist empire which had already been established, the U.S.S.R. Thus, the New Deal saved Stalin from internal collapse by extending diplomatic recognition and thereby helped him obtain loans which tided him over.[1] More recently, we have witnessed the ratification of the Nuclear Test Ban Treaty following a pressure campaign on the Senate of almost unparalleled intensity by the Kennedy-Johnson Administration. And this despite the blunt warning of responsible military leaders and Dr. Edward Teller himself, father of the hydrogen bomb, that such a treaty would only work to the benefit of the Russians, whose leader has sworn to bury us.[2] In addition, we have the unbroken record of Soviet Russia in breaking treaties.

The second line of attack launched by the liberal establishment, as it has been called, was against business and industry. The concept became ingrained in several generations of college students that profit was evil. Business was openly harassed. A double standard came into being—one set of rules restricting and hamstringing business while another set bestowed power and unlimited monopoly upon socialist labor leaders like Walter Reuther, who is a vice president of the NAACP. Business and industry were taxed unmercifully to provide the funds for still more government spending, while at the same time they were stifled by regulations as the insatiable thirst for power of those in control in Washington grew apace.

The third line of attack in the revolution against our established social and economic system was the most devilish of all. It was an attack upon the race which had developed the most advanced and most highly industrialized country in the world. Under the idealistically glowing phrases of "brotherhood" and "tolerance" all races were to be submerged in a sea of equalitarianism through integration. And all were to be ruled by a liberal "elite" in a planned society. . . .

Let us now consider how the attack on racial integrity—or social

---

[1]This statement is pure fiction. The Soviet Union apparently sought recognition from the United States government as a step in achieving national security, especially against Japan. Negotiations for an international loan, at the time of United States recognition, were unsuccessful. See Barrington Moore Jr., *Soviet Politics—The Dilemma of Power* (New York, 1965), p. 359; and Max Beloff, *The Foreign Policy of Soviet Russia, 1929-41* (London, 1947), Vol. I, p. 122.

[2]General Maxwell Taylor, then chairman of the Joint Chiefs of Staff, testified before the Senate Foreign Relations Committee that the Nuclear Test Ban Treaty was "in the national interest." See *New York Times*, August 16, 1963, p. 1.

separation of the races—under the slogan of *CIVIL RIGHTS* is closely connected with the attack on our constitutional freedoms.

It comes about in this fashion. The [federal] government is today controlled by liberals or collectivists, or welfare staters, or whatever. Now why is this group able to maintain itself in power? Because primarily of the fact that the white conservatives are divided into conflicting political and sectional groups and the white liberals hold the balance of power through the leverage of the negro bloc vote. This is obvious in the heavy voting Northern states, and it is coming to be more of a factor in the North, for instance, that elected the present Democratic Administration. Hence the combined drive by the Administration and the negro pressure groups to force Southern states to register hundreds of thousands of unqualified negroes.

To get this bloc vote, the liberals promise more and more special privileges for negroes in the form of "civil rights" bills, which not only would give them social and political preference, but economic as well.

The only way in which politicians have ever held the negro bloc vote is through an ever ascending rate of taxing whites and spending on negroes. Of all aspects of the welfare state, this is one of the most immoral, for it subsidizes laziness and waste at the expense of industry and thrift. Such brazen redistribution of the wealth amounts to no less than stealing. It takes from those who have earned and gives to those who have not. . . .

[Richard D. Morphew]

The basic question in the Mississippi crisis[3] was—and remains—this: Whether a contract called the Constitution of the United States means what is says, or whether the power of centralized authority shall be able to overcome this contract at will.

People in Mississippi and California and the other states agree on one point: The laws legally enacted by Congress and the Constitution of the United States should be obeyed. The rub comes when someone acts without legal or constitutional basis, then claims that *his* will must be obeyed instead of the Constitution.

The Constitution of the United States is the contract whereby the sovereign states of our nation—there are now 50 of them—delegate to

---

[3]Morphew was speaking in the aftermath of the crisis occasioned by the enrollment of James Meredith, a Negro, in the University of Mississippi. Because of threats of widespread violence, President John F. Kennedy dispatched 30,000 troops to the campus over the strenuous objections of Governor Ross Barnett and other Mississippi authorities. A riot ensued causing two deaths and numerous injuries.

the Federal government certain specific powers, such as those necessary for defense, carrying on foreign affairs, coining money, and so forth. These powers are listed in the Constitution. Then, there follows a specific statement:

> The powers not delegated to the United States by the Constitution, nor prohibited by it to the States, are reserved to the States respectively, or to the people.

This is the Tenth Amendment in the Bill of Rights.

So the issue should really be quite simple. Does the Constitution delegate to the Federal government any power to impose its will in regard to educational systems operated by a state? No!

Are states prohibited by the Constitution from running their own schools in their own way? No!

Has Congress passed a law to require any of the things which are being forced at bayonet-point on Mississippi? No!

If those who favor centralized control want to, can they propose a Constitutional Amendment to make things work their way? Yes!

Have they proposed such an Amendment and had it properly ratified? No!

Then shouldn't we be bound by what the Constitution says? Yes!

With these questions clear, then, what is happening? The appointed members of the Supreme Court have determined without law and without authority under the Constitution to impose their will upon the states. They act as legislators in making their own decrees; they act as executives in seeking to carry them out.

In Mississippi, this action ran head-on into a determined governor, backed by an unquestioned majority of the people, all of whom believe that the Constitution and the law do not allow what the courts are attempting to force. Since the actions of the courts are without legal authority, the people of Mississippi will not accept them.[4]

---

[4]The Supreme Court declared racial segregation in public education unconstitutional in *Brown* v. *Board of Education* (1954), citing the provision in the 14th Amendment which declared that "No state shall . . . deny to any person within its jurisdiction equal protection of the laws." Meredith's enrollment was pursuant to a valid federal court order in the case of *Meredith* v. *Fair.* Precedents for the President's dispatch of troops without the invitation of state authorities included George Washington's use of militia forces to put down the Whiskey Rebellion in Pennsylvania in 1794; Grover Cleveland's dispatch of federal troops to enforce a federal court injunction in the Pullman strike of 1895; and President Eisenhower's dispatch of troops to Little Rock in 1957. In upholding Cleveland's actions the Supreme Court said *(In re Debs):* "The entire strength of the nation may be used to enforce in any part of the land the full and free exercise of all national powers and the security of all rights entrusted by the Constitution to its care. . . . If the emergency arises, the army of the Nation, and all its militia, are at the service of the Nation to compel obedience to its laws." Quoted in James Silver, *Mississippi: The Closed Society* (New York, 1964), p. 140.

Seemingly, then, the situation had reached an impasse. Let us consider for a moment if any action might have been taken to resolve matters while upholding the processes of constitutional government. Can there be a fair solution to this problem, one which reasonable men on both sides could find acceptable?

My answer is an emphatic *yes*—although I hasten to qualify it by saying that I can't realistically expect the advocates of Federal force to accept it. They would far rather use centralized power to overcome the Constitution.

But there is an alternative that would wash away all shadow of doubt about illegality and unconstitutionality. There is a way to provide a constitutional answer which persons on both sides could accept in good faith.

Here's how the question could be resolved with justice. At present, the Constitution clearly does not provide for the Federal government to intervene in educational matters. These affairs are left to the states and to the people. So let's deal with this question by constitutional means!

Let those who uphold the Federal position propose an Amendment to the Constitution of the United States to allow—without a shadow of a doubt—Federal control over education. Such an Amendment must win a two-thirds vote in both the House and the Senate; then it must be ratified by three-fourths of the states to become a part of the Constitution.

Frankly, I would oppose such an Amendment. I do not think it would stand a chance of being adopted. But if it were legally adopted as part of the Constitution, then it would legally become "the law of the land," and would be upheld as such.

However, if such an Amendment should fail, then the American people would have spoken, and Federal harassment and aggression of the states on matters of education should be dropped forever.

Why hasn't this approach been tried? Simply because some persons in high places are not interested in constitutional government and good will. They are unwilling to take their chances through democratic processes. They prefer to use the centralized force at their command to impose their will, without regard for the Constitution!

And that's exactly what's been done in Mississippi! So many provisions of the Constitution have been violated during the current military occupation of the Oxford, Mississippi area that it would probably be faster to cite the provisions which haven't been shattered. . . .

Less than three weeks ago, the police state came to America! And they didn't even bother to declare martial law!

All this despite the Constitution of the United States—the solemn contract on which our existence as a free people depends.

Article IV, Section 4 of the Constitution says:

The United States shall guarantee to every State in this Union a republican form of government, and shall protect each of them against invasion; and on application of the Legislature, or of the executive (when the Legislature cannot be convened) against domestic violence.

There is no provision whatsoever in the Constitution for sending Federal troops into a state, except on application of the Legislature, or of the governor if the Legislature can't be convened. Now Mississippi's Legislature was in session—and it certainly didn't request any troops! Governor Barnett didn't ask for any! So obviously, the sending of Federal troops to Mississippi was a plain violation of the Constitution. This is aggression in its simplest form.

The Bill of Rights has been violated wholesale. Freedom of speech and of assembly were trampled beneath paratroopers' boots on the Ole Miss campus, the First Amendment notwithstanding.

The Second Amendment guarantees that "the right of the people to keep and bear arms shall not be infringed." Yet, everything from BB guns to rocks of throwable size were seized at military roadblocks.

The Fourth Amendment is supposed to protect us from unreasonable searches and seizures. But the soldiers in Oxford laughed if anyone mentioned a search warrant—or they prodded you with a bayonet, depending on the mood they were in.

The Eighth Amendment states that excessive bail, excessive fines, and cruel and unusual punishment are prohibited. How can this be squared with the atrocity reports?

Of course, the Ninth and Tenth Amendments, giving certain rights to the states and the people, were again trampled wantonly.

And even the illegally-adopted Fourteenth Amendment, cited by the Warren Court as grounds for outlawing racial segregation, can cut both ways. In all the turmoil over getting James Meredith into Ole Miss, what about the rights of the 5,000 legitimate students who were already there in pursuit of an education? This was of no concern to the marshals and troops. Yet, the Fourteenth Amendment guarantees "equal protection of the laws."

In fact, about the only part of the Constitution still in effect in Mississippi is the Sixteenth Amendment—the one which permits us to pay the income tax.

Of course, some may say that the situation at Oxford was serious, and that, therefore, the Constitution just couldn't be bothered with. There's no question that the situation was serious—but what made it that way was previous violations of the Constitution.

There's an old saying that one thing leads to another. This has certainly been true in the Mississippi crisis. One violation of the Constitution has led to another, and another, and another . . . until some violations are now being used to justify still more violations.

If you'll stop to think about it, you'll realize that this is the way free governments are destroyed. This is the way constitutional rights and law are cast aside. Some countries in this troubled world could testify that this is the way dictatorship fastens its control upon the people.

That is why it's so important that all of us—we in Mississippi and you in California and others throughout the nation—be ever on the alert, seeing to it that our country's constitutional and legal principles be upheld scrupulously. The real issue is not whether one Negro shall be enrolled in the University of Mississippi. That has been settled. He will remain at Ole Miss only so long as his bodyguards—the troops and marshals—remain. When they leave, Meredith leaves—and he knows it![5] . . .

But in the Mississippi crisis, if Meredith's enrollment is not the big issue . . . if continued segregation is not the pervading question . . . then what is?

Simply this: the issue is one of dictatorial power versus the constitutional rights of the people. Despite pious protestations to the contrary, the Federal action against Mississippi violated the Constitution in a number of ways; therefore, those who dictated it must bear responsibility for the horrible results.

Those who speak of the Federal aggression in terms of "law" cannot cite a single section of the Constitution, a single act passed by Congress, or a single treaty that provides them any basis for their emotional, vote-buying, revolutionary position.

The Constitution does not say that a decree by a court—*any* court—

---

[5]This of course did not occur. Meredith's "bodyguards" were soon withdrawn and Meredith remained to graduate. Since his enrollment several dozen Negro students have enrolled, all peacefully, at the University of Mississippi.

is "the law of the land." If it were, Americans would live in a dictatorship, for our Federal judiciary is appointed and therefore unresponsive to the people. We would be at the unmerciful mercy of a panel of nine dictators on the Supreme Court who could rule as they willed, and demand Federal force to carry out their orders against an enslaved populace.

The Mississippi tragedy has resulted from political, sociological and demagogic substitution of the decrees of appointed men for law. So when President Kennedy and his partisans speak of upholding "the law," they still find themselves without any law to cite. Thus they expose their hypocrisy and their willingness to take into their own hands powers which are not theirs, all this despite the fact that the President took a solemn oath to "preserve, protect and defend the Constitution of the United States."

By failing to preserve, protect and defend the Constitution—by substituting dictatorship for it—the President has infringed upon the rights of the States and the people.

For if a mere court decree may upset the Constitution, the law, and previous court rulings on this kind of question which have stood for generations, then what is to prohibit appointed dictators from depriving all Americans of all their freedoms?

If these changes can be wrought contrary to the Constitution and to the law, what is to prevent some appointed court from ruling, for example, that in its "interpretation" of the Constitution, Americans may have free speech—only if the freedom is not extended to criticism of whatever rulers may be in power?

What is to keep appointed judges, if they succeed now, from ruling that freedom of religion may be retained only to the extent of bowing at whatever altar that dictators may designate?

As one portion of freedom goes, so all may go, if we let it!

This issue of Federal usurpation is vital to freedom because it is the weapon whereby freedom in America today is most threatened with destruction. No external enemy, Communist or any other, so endangers Americans as does unconstitutional government within our nation.

As our enemies rejoice at our misery, let us as Americans seek the course that may yet save our nation.

All of us deplore violence and the situations which create it. But we must do more than that! We must raise a standard of reason and information to enable our people—through the democratic processes—

to undo the injustices that have been dictatorially committed, preserving both freedom and the peace.

Let us recognize, as did Jefferson, that "The God who gave us life, gave us liberty at the same time."

Let us strive, as did Jefferson, to "Enlighten the people generally, and tyranny and oppressions of body and mind will vanish like evil spirits at the dawn of day."

Finally, let us, along with Jefferson, "swear upon the altar of God eternal hostility against every form of tyranny over the mind of man."

We shall thus realize what the Founding Fathers must have known. In the clarion words of Patrick Henry, "We are not weak if we make a proper use of those means which the God of Nature has placed in our power. . . . The battle, sir, is not to the strong alone, it is to the vigilant, the active, the brave!"

Epilogue: A Rebuttal to Segregationists

It seems unnecessary to rebut each error and distortion in the materials reprinted in this collection. Most of them are obvious, even to the casual reader. It is also obvious that the segregationist argument rests largely upon assumptions and value judgments rather than concrete, empirical data. For this reason much of it defies objective refutation. Like religion, it is acceptable only to those who have faith and the will to believe.

Consider, for example, the "science" of segregationists, the most systematic element in their ideology. It is structured around a basic fallacy, a misunderstanding of the concept of race. Scientific racists believe *race* is a fixed, permanent entity through which an individual inherits not only distinctive physical features, but equally distinctive and far more important mental, moral, and behavioral traits. There exist, then, or so segregationists contend, such things as "Negro intelligence," "Negro morality," and "Negro personality," which are racially (i.e., genetically) predetermined in the same manner as skin color, hair texture, and facial configuration. These entities constitute the "racial psychology" described above by James Bardin. They also reflect the *quality* of the Negro race, according to segregationists, a quality which can be measured by the culture Negroes produce, the society they create, the morality they display, the intellectual levels they attain. In each of these areas, segregationists believe, Negro achievement is vastly inferior to that of whites, and they conclude from this that races are unequal and Negroes inferior. Racial averages and not individual excellence, they insist, are the proper criteria for measurement; individual Negroes are Negroes first and then individuals.

A logical consequence of these ideas is Professor Thomas' thesis, reprinted above, that race prejudice and "consciousness of kind" are instincts. Here is an effectual example of how an assumption (that races differ psychologically) leads segregationists to a conclusion (that race prejudice is instinctive) which to them acquires the coloration of fact. By its nature the conclusion is difficult to disprove empirically; that it is fallacious, however, seems apparent. Not all persons are racially prejudiced, and those who are differ widely in the intensity of their prejudice. Historically whites have perhaps exhibited more prejudice of the type Professor Thomas described than have Negroes, but their prejudice has varied notably from time to time and place to place. Furthermore, if "consciousness of kind" is an instinct, it seems paradoxical that segregationists are forced to such lengths to preserve segregation. By their logic racial separation should be voluntary and relatively complete. Intervenors in the *Stell* case illustrate the contradictions of segregationists on this point. They note that "selective associational or racial preference is a universal human trait" and use it to explain the "increase in social tension and interracial friction" which they say inevitably accompanies school integration. Yet, among the consequences they foresaw of school integration in Savannah were increases in "interracial social intercourse, interracial dating, interracial dancing, etc."

There are still other fallacies in the segregationists' use of racial psychology. There *are* important racial differences in "psychology" and behavior. Negroes in America *do,* on the average, make consistently lower scores than whites on intelligence, aptitude, and achievement tests. They *do,* on the average, commit more of certain crimes and have higher rates of illegitimacy and venereal disease. They *do* have more broken homes and rundown neighborhoods. They *do* often deviate from middle-class ideals of conduct. African civilization *is* "inferior" to that of Europe in such things as modern technology. By themselves, however, these statements are meaningless or misleading. The significant point is not whether these conditions exist, but rather their meaning, their cause, their cure. Segregationists blame them on race. To do so, however, is no more logical than blaming race for similar behavior patterns among Caucasians. For example, Caucasians seem to commit a disproportionate share of white-collar crimes; and Northerners tend on the average to score higher than Southerners on IQ tests.[1] To suggest that these conditions are racial rather than environmental is ludicrous. Yet, a racial

---

[1]See for example Horace Mann Bond's review of Audrey Shuey's *The Testing of Negro Intelligence* (Lynchburg, Va., 1958) in "Cat on a Hot Tin Roof," *Journal of Negro Education,* Vol. XXVII (Fall, 1958), pp. 519-23. Miss Shuey had collected data from psychological test results to prove that Negroes are innately less intelligent than whites. Bond, using the relevant portions of Miss Shuey's evidence, found just as much proof that northern whites are innately superior in intelligence to southern whites.

explanation for similar conditions among Negroes is generally accepted by segregationists. It suits their purposes, and they find it easy to defend. One need only look around, they insist, to see the importance of race and the differences it produces between whites and Negroes. These differences, whether of physical features, IQ test scores, or personal behavior, are, in the eyes of segregationists, the meaning and manifestation of race.

To scientists and social scientists today, *race* is not nearly so powerful or static a force. It is instead a "process, a series of temporary genetic conditions always in process of change." They define races as "populations which differ in the relative commonness of some of their genes," or as "genetically isolated mating groups with distinctive gene frequencies."[2] Thus, races differ relatively, not absolutely, and the difference is in the frequency of certain genes. Genes (and the chromosomes which contain them) are the mechanisms of heredity, but they are not racial in nature. "Negro genes" do not differ in kind from "white genes." An individual Negro does not inherit a set of "Negro genes" which, by racist logic, would give him "Negro intelligence," "Negro personality," and "Negro morality." Intelligence, personality, and morality are influenced to some unknown but considerable degree by heredity; however, the influence operates on an individual rather than a racial basis. In every race there is a vast reservoir of genes of which an individual inherits only a minute percentage. Every individual (except identical twins), regardless of race, has his own special gene combination and is a unique human being. His traits and abilities are his as an individual, not as a Negro or Caucasian. There is probably complete overlap of personality and morality types, as well as range of mental ability, among basic racial groups. The range of individual differences within each race is far greater than average differences between races.

Nor is the genetic composition of a race static.[3] In the case of American Negroes there has always been a steady infusion of "Caucasian genes" so that perhaps one-fourth of the Negro's gene pool

[2]Ashley Montagu, *Man in Process* (New York, 1961, pp. 91-92; L. C. Dunn and Theodosius Dobzhansky, *Heredity, Race and Society* (New York, 1946), p. 108; and Thomas F. Pettigrew, *A Profile of the Negro American* (Princeton, N.J.: Princeton University Press, 1964), pp. 100-35.

[3]This and related subjects are explained in layman's terms in Theodosius Dobzhansky, *The Biological Basis of Human Freedom* (New York, 1958); Theodosius Dobzhansky, *Mankind Evolving* (New Haven, Conn.: Yale University Press, 1962); and Ashley Montagu (ed.), *The Concept of Race* (New York, 1964).

today consists of "alien genes." (The same is also true of whites, though the degree of Negro intermixture is much less since everyone with recognizable Negro features is considered a "Negro.") This pointedly illustrates the differences between biological and social definitions of race. Natural selection, mutation, and genetic drift also operate to alter the genetic composition of racial groups, and thereby contribute decisively to the dynamic of race, to the constant re-shuffling and recombination of genes, to the "process" mentioned above.

Besides misconstruing the nature of race and inheritance, segregationists also misunderstand intelligence, which is vastly more complicated and fascinating than they believe. They look upon intelligence, as upon race, as fixed and static, and in large measure racially determined. But the evidence is massive and wholly convincing that it is individual and plastic.[4] "Intelligence is not merely an inherited capacity, genetically fixed and destined to unfold in a biologically predetermined manner," Harvard psychologist Thomas F. Pettigrew has written. "It is a dynamic, on-going set of processes that within wide hereditary limits is subject to innumerable experiential factors." According to studies cited by Professor Pettigrew, intelligence is affected by such diverse environmental factors as the diet of the mother during pregnancy, home life, cultural opportunities, especially during early childhood, personality, personal ambition, racial discrimination, and "role-playing" by Negroes. Other scholars have offered similar evidence, equally damaging to segregationists' views. It must be admitted that the evidence of equalitarian social scientists is not yet definitive, that is, they have not proved objectively that races are equal in intelligence. They have, however, demonstrated that environment is a pervasive influence upon IQ test scores and intellectual achievement.

The segregationists' view of intelligence parallels Robert Bennett Bean's description of the Negro brain. Bean's study is one of the most widely cited items in the literature of scientific racism, and logically so for it reflects many typical features of segregationist "science." Bean's enthusiasm exceeded both his knowledge of Negro

---

[4]See for example Pettigrew, *op. cit.*, pp. 100-35. See also Otto Klineberg, "Negro-White Differences in Intelligence Test Performance: A New Look at an Old Problem," *American Psychologist*, Vol. XVIII (April, 1963), pp. 198-203; Ralph M. Dreger and Kent S. Miller, "Comparative Psychological Studies of Negroes and Whites in the United States," *Psychological Bulletin*, Vol. LVII, No. 5 (1960), pp. 361-402; Otto Klineberg, *Race Differences* (New York, 1935); and J. McV. Hunt, *Intelligence and Experience* (New York, 1961).

brains and his awareness of the limitations of science. As a result, his study is now dismissed by all social scientists except a few who are dedicated segregationists. Physiologist Dwight J. Ingle of the University of Chicago recently reviewed Bean's study and pointed out its deficiencies:

How should the claim of genetic inferiority of the Negro brain be tested? It would be necessary to gather representative samples of brains from different races in which environment, including prenatal and postnatal nutrition, was equivalent. The factors of age and health would have to be controlled. The brains would have to be removed from skulls at the same time after death, fixed, processed and measured by identical methods, and then studied as "unknowns" by not one but several experts. If it were possible to establish significant average differences in brains among races, it would remain to be shown that any difference is a mark of inferiority, or that it is a physical measure of intellect or other quality of mind. Claims to knowledge must also withstand replication of the experiments supplying the evidence as well as debate and criticism of the design of the study, the technical details, and the interpretation of data. Such studies have not been made for the simple reason that they are not possible.[5]

Bean's study met none of these criteria. "There is no objective evidence," Ingle declared, "that any of the average differences claimed to exist [by Bean and others] are marks of inferiority or correlate with intelligence and behavior.

Bean's study typifies the transcendent weakness of segregationist "science": its authorities invariably read anti-Negro biases into their data and conclusions. Convinced that races are unequal and Negroes are inferior to whites, they use science and social science to "prove" that "fact." The result is diabolical—science is exploited for racist ends—though the purpose, often, is not. On the contrary, most scientific racists seek to rescue racial policy from the grip of demagogues and place it in the hands of rational, disinterested men of science. Their efforts are abortive, however, for they are prisoners of their own racism. The policies they advocate differ little in substance from those of demagogues.

This fact is pointedly illustrated in the discussions of Negro education by Professor Odum and Bishop Bratton. Certainly in their own minds both men were motivated by a desire to help Negroes. Yet the help they offered only exacerbated the problems of the race. At the

---

[5]Dwight J. Ingle, "Comments on the Teachings of Carleton Putnam," *Mankind Quarterly*, Vol. IV (1963), p. 30.

time Odum and Bratton wrote, in the early 20th century, Negroes were surely in need of more and better education, but the education they advocated would neither enlighten nor emancipate the race. Nor would it make Negroes self-reliant, equal citizens. It would instead teach them to accept segregation and train them to be useful laborers in the white man's service. It would, in short, buttress southern race policies, strengthen white supremacy, and further mire the race in the slough of segregation and inequality. Neither Odum nor Bratton was concerned with intellectual training; each was convinced that the Negro mind is incapable of "higher" development. Negroes "educated" in their system would be "good niggers" in the parlance of southern whites, but if they were intelligent human beings it was in spite of not because of their education. Their Negro students would learn little because they would be taught little; they would be taught little because no one believed them capable of learning. Thus the segregationists' prophecy was self-fulfilling. By their control of education, segregationists molded Negroes to fit their stereotype of the race. They then complained of the Negro's lack of intelligence and low IQ scores, and used both as proof of Negro inferiority and justification for racial segregation.

The weakness and disrepute of segregationist "science" today are easily illustrated. In 1961, the Society for the Psychological Study of Social Issues, a subdivision of the American Psychological Association, adopted a statement which read in part:

> There are differences in intelligence test scores when one compares a random sample of whites and Negroes. What is equally clear is that no evidence exists that leads to the conclusion that such differences are innate. Quite to the contrary, the evidence points overwhelmingly to the fact that when one compares Negroes and whites of comparable cultural and educational background, differences in intelligence diminish markedly; the more comparable the background, the less the difference. There is no direct evidence that supports the view that there is an innate difference between members of different racial groups.[6]

In 1962, the American Association of Physical Anthropologists endorsed the following statement:

> We, the members of the American Association of Physical Anthropologists, professionally concerned with differences in man, deplore the misuse of science to advocate racism. . . .

---

[6]"Statement on Race and Intelligence from the Society for the Psychological Study of Social Issues," *Perspectives in Biology and Medicine,* Vol. V (Autumn, 1961), p. 129.

. . . We affirm, as we have in the past, that there is nothing in science that justifies the denial of opportunities or rights to any group by virtue of race.[7]

In 1961, the American Anthropological Association adopted a resolution on the same subject:

The American Anthropological Association repudiates statements now appearing in the United States that Negroes are biologically and in innate mental ability inferior to whites, and reaffirms the fact that there is no scientifically established evidence to justify the exclusion of any race from the rights guaranteed by the Constitution of the United States. The basic principles of equality of opportunity and equality before the law are compatible with all that is known about human biology. All races possess the abilities needed to participate fully in the democratic way of life and in modern technological civilization.[8]

Finally, the Society for the Study of Social Problem, a division of the American Sociological Association endorsed the same view in 1961:

. . . The great preponderance of scientific opinion has favored the conclusion that there is little or no ground on which to assume that the racial groups in question are innately different in any important human capacity. . . . The conclusion of scientists is that the differences in test performance by members of so-called racial groups are due not to racial but to environmental factors. This is the operating assumption today of the vast majority of the competent scientists in the field.[9]

As these statements indicate, a major fallacy in the logic of scientific racists is their insistence that race relations and Negro rights are genetic issues best understood in light of the Negro's genetic inheritance and evolutionary development. In point of fact, however, they are social and political issues to be resolved within the context of the Constitution and Bill of Rights, the precepts of American democracy, and the realities of national politics. American Negroes are what they are today because of environmental and historical factors, not racial deficiencies. They are also American citizens, not racial abstractions, with the same rights, liberties, and responsibilities of other citizens.

---

[7]"American Physical Anthropologists Condemn Racism," *Current Anthropology*, Vol. III (October, 1962), p. 445.

[8]"Science and Segregation: The American Anthropological Association Dips into Politics," *Science*, Vol. CXXXIV (December 8, 1961), pp. 1868-69.

[9]Quoted in Pettigrew, *op. cit.*, p. 134.

Our racial policies must incorporate that fact. Of course science is relevant to the formulation of race policies, and other public policies, too, for that matter. It can illuminate issues and assist statesmen in their search for truth, but it is their servant, not their master.

The same is true of religion. The rights of Negroes as American citizens are no more dependent upon the "curse of Canaan" or "God's plan" in creating separate races than upon IQ test scores, cephalic indexes, or convolutions of the brain. Here in fact is one of the ironies of segregationist thought. Segregationists invariably pose as strict constitutionalists, and criticize their opponents for advocating racial policies not consistent with the letter of the Constitution. However, they often insist that the Constitution be interpreted to suit their own science and religion.

The religious ideas of segregationists are not so much "wrong" as they are irrelevant. Religion is a personal thing; it rests ultimately upon faith and personal conviction, upon emotion and the heart rather than reason or objective evidence. But this is true for equalitarians, as well as segregationists, and the former use God, Christianity, and the Bible in formulating and defending racial views remarkably different from those of the latter. It is pointless to say that segregationists have misread the Bible or misconstrued the Christian message. It is more meaningful to note that there is little biblical scholarship to support their interpretation of specific scriptures. For example, the biblical story most widely cited as authority for Negro inferiority and racial segregation is that of the "curse of Canaan." Historian David Brion Davis of Cornell University, who recently made an exhaustive study of the sources of Western attitudes toward slavery, has written of the curse of Canaan (it was also widely used by antebellum Southerners to defend slavery):

In view of the significance attached to Noah's curse by later apologists for Negro slavery, we might note that the passage, while giving divine sanction to slavery as a punishment, is filled with complexities and inconsistencies. According to Gerhard Von Rad, the original Yahwistic narrative had nothing to do with Shem, Ham, and Japheth, and the ecumenical scheme of nations which follows. It was rather an older story, limited to the Palestinian Shem, Japheth, and Canaan, and connected with the horror felt by the newly arrived Israelites at the sexual depravity of the Canaanites. Later on, a redacter inserted the name Ham as the father of Canaan, in an effort to harmonize the narrative with the later table of nations (Genesis, a Commentary [tr. by John H. Marks, Philadelphia, 1961], pp. 131-33). This provided the basis for elaborate exegesis designed to prove that Negroes, being descended from Ham, were meant to be slaves.[10]

The "history" of segregationists has the same deficiencies as their religion and science. As historians, segregationists were principally concerned with African civilization and 19th-century America, and in neither area has their scholarship stood the test of time. It should be remembered, however, that the historical views they endorsed were until World War II generally accepted by historians and the American public. Americans of both races knew little and cared perhaps less about Africa, and whites had little interest in Negro history. They did, however, have considerable interest in *Negroes in history*. They regard history as a source of authority for their racial views, and they used it accordingly. They exploited history in the same manner they used science. They sought not historical truth but evidence of Negro inferiority and justification for segregation. In fact, their history is so permeated with anti-Negro views that its validity stands or falls on those views. Convinced that Negroes are incapable of creating a civilization, they considered it axiomatic that Africa had no civilization or culture worthy of the name. Whatever existed in the "dark continent" was—must be—barbarism and savagery. Their standard of measurement was European, Caucasian. In their view Europe's civilization *was* civilization, and insofar as Africa differed from Europe, Africa was inferior. The concept of cultural relativism was unknown or meaningless to them. As a consequence, they closed their minds to the complexities and subtleties of African civilization and to the achievements and accomplishments of the African people. The result was additional "evidence" of Negro inferiority and further "justification" for segregation. But it was not history.

A brief quotation from a recent work by historian August Meier and sociologist Elliott M. Rudwick indicates something of the development of African civilization at the time of the slave trade:

West African societies in the slaving area ranged from small tribes to large kingdoms of a million or more; from small groups where kinships ties were the source of all authority to large states with complex political institutions. These societies were characterized by economic specialization and a monetary system based on cowrie shell to facilitate trade. The larger ones had a system of social classes and a hierarchical territorial political organization. Interlacing and under-

---

[10]David Brion Davis, *The Problem of Slavery in Western Culture* (Ithaca, N.Y.: Cornell University Press, 1966), pp. 63-64n.

pinning these political, economic, and social class arrangements were a deeply rooted and intricate kinship system extending from family to clan, and an elaborate web of religious belief, involving an individual, the kinship groupings, and the entire society.[11]

Concerning the question of whether Negroes ever originated any civilization of their own, Professors Meier and Rudwick wrote as follows:

Modern scholarship places the western Sudan [the broad area of western Africa south of the Sahara and north of the Guinea coast and the Congo river basin] among the important creative centers in the development of human culture—along with the Ancient Near East, the Indus and Yellow river valleys, and Meso-America. In each of these areas an unusually high agricultural productivity achieved during the Neolithic period sustained a relatively dense population and thus ultimately led to a profound transformation in social institutions. In each case the social complexities arising out of the increasing number of inhabitants resulted in the development of social classes, urban centers, and despotic theocratic monarchies.[12]

The segregationists' treatment of 19th-century American history is no better than their treatment of Africa. The validity of Philip Alexander Bruce's justification of southern race policies and Claude Bowers' description of Radical Reconstruction, for example, rests in large part upon the validity of their assumptions that Negroes are inferior to whites, that they cannot make responsible American citizens, that segregation and white supremacy are essential public policies, and that social equality and racial intermarriage are horrors to be avoided at all cost. Were these assumptions true, the history of Bruce and Bowers might be valid. Since they are not, their history has little merit.

However, the deficiencies of segregationist historians are greater than the weakness of their initial assumptions. The facts of 19th-century American history, as now known, make their interpretations largely untenable. The research of historians over the last generation has destroyed the authority of Bowers' view that the Reconstruction Radicals were a group of crafty, malevolent conspirators motivated entirely by selfish political and economic interests or sheer vindictiveness toward the prostrate white South. It is now clear that

---

[11]August Meier and Elliott M. Rudwick, *From Plantation to Ghetto* (New York, 1966), p. 10.

[12]*Ibid.,* p. 5.

the Radicals were as diverse (and as "good" or "bad") as any other significant political group in 19th-century America; that the reforms they sponsored in defense of Negro rights (notably the 14th and 15th Amendments, the Civil Rights Acts of 1866 and 1875, the Force Bill, and the Freedmen's Bureau) were generally reasonable and sometimes farsighted; that "Black Reconstruction" was not "black" at all since Negroes never controlled Reconstruction policy anywhere; that Reconstruction thus proves nothing about the capability of Negroes for responsible citizenship; that the Reconstruction governments were no more corrupt or financially irresponsible than the national government of the Grant administration or the white "Redeemer" governments which replaced the Radical governments in the South; that the opposition of President Andrew Johnson, the southern whites, and others to Radical Reconstruction was in part due to their belief in Negro inferiority and their consequent determination to preserve white supremacy in the South. "The Fourteenth and Fifteenth Amendments were now part of the federal Constitution," historian Kenneth Stampp has written, summarizing the accomplishments of Radical Reconstruction.

As a result, Negroes could no longer be deprived of the right to vote, except by extralegal coercion or by some devious subterfuge. They could not be deprived of equal civil rights, except by deceit. They could not be segregated in public places, except by the spurious argument that this did not in fact deprive them of the equal protection of the laws. Thus Negroes were no longer denied equality by the plain language of the law, as they had been before radical reconstruction, but only by coercion, by subterfuge, by deceit, and by spurious legalism.

The 14th and 15th Amendments, Professor Stampp continues, "could have been adopted only under the conditions of radical reconstruction," and such worthy achievements cause "the blunders of that era tragic though they were, [to] dwindle into insignificance. For if it was worth four years of civil war to save the Union, it was worth a few years of radical reconstruction to give the American Negro the ultimate promise of equal civil and political rights."[13] And, in the final analysis, it was the protection accorded Negroes which led segregationists to look with such horror upon the Radicals and their Reconstruction program.

---

[13]Kenneth Stampp, *The Era of Reconstruction, 1865-1877* (New York, 1965), pp. 214-15.

To speculate upon the future of segregationist thought is dangerous at best. Emotional subjects rarely follow a rational historical course. The ideas of anti-Negro racism have varied considerably over the years; yet the major thrust of segregationist thought remained remarkably consistent. Many white Americans still believe innate racial differences (or inequalities) are so great that whites and Negroes must occupy different places in American life. It seems logical to expect they will continue to believe so until circumstances force them to change their minds. Historically, segregationists have been notable for their intransigence, and other whites for their indifference to the plight of Negroes. For these reasons Negro militancy and Negro achievement would seem to be the most efficacious means of affecting fundamental changes in segregationist thinking as well as racial policy.

Bibliographical Essay

Segregationist thought is best approached through the writings of segregationists and white supremacists. Those writings are numerous and varied, and only a few representative examples can be mentioned here. The views of the more extreme segregationists are expressed in such works as William P. Calhoun, *The Caucasian and the Negro in the United States* (Columbia, S.C., 1902); John Ambrose Price, *The Negro Past, Present, and Future* (New York, 1907); E. H. Randle, *Characteristics of the Southern Negro* (New York, 1910); William Benjamin Smith, *The Color Line, A Brief in Behalf of the Unborn* (New York, 1905); R. W. Shufeldt, *America's Greatest Problem: The Negro* (Philadelphia, 1915); Earnest Sevier Cox, *White America* (Richmond, 1923); and James Denson Sayers, *Can the White Race Survive?* (Washington, 1929).

More moderate and paternalistic views are stated in such works as Thomas Nelson Page, *The Negro: The Southerner's Problem* (New York, 1904); Howard Odum, *Social and Mental Traits of the Negro* (New York, 1910); and Thomas Pearce Bailey, *Race Orthodoxy in the South* (New York, 1914). George Oscar Ferguson, *The Psychology of the Negro, An Experimental Study* (New York, 1916) and Marion J. Mayo, *The Mental Capacity of the American Negro* (New York, 1913) are representative of the many works of scientific racism of the first quarter of this century. The varied aspects of religious racism are reflected in William Montgomery Brown, *The Crucial Race Question* (Little Rock, 1907) and Robert Edwin Smith, *Christianity and the Race Problem* (New York, 1922). Thomas Dixon's many novels, for example, *The Leopard's Spots, A Romance of the White Man's Burden* (New York, 1902) and *The Clansman, An Historical Romance of the Ku Klux Klan* (New York, 1905), illustrate the manner in which anti-Negro racism sometimes intruded itself into works of fiction. *The Clansman* was the basis for the famous D. W. Griffith film, *The Birth of a Nation.*

The defense of segregation and white supremacy by Southern politicians fills the pages of the *Congressional Record.* Many of the

176

politicians have written works summarizing their racial views. For representative examples see Oscar W. Underwood, "The Negro Problem in the South," *Forum,* Vol. XXX (October, 1900), pp. 215-19; F. M. Simmons, "The Political Future of the South," *Independent,* Vol. LX (June 28, 1906), pp. 1521-26; Theodore Bilbo, *Take Your Choice: Separation or Mongrelization* (Poplarville, Miss., 1947); and Herman Talmadge, *You and Segregation* (Birmingham, 1955). *The Citizens' Council* (1955-61) and *The Citizen* (1962-   ), official publications of the Citizens' Councils of America (headquarters: Jackson, Mississippi) are excellent sources of segregationist thought in the years since the *Brown* v. *Board of Education* decision. More systematic expressions of contemporary segregationist thought are found in Carleton Putnam, *Race and Reason* (Washington, 1961); Putnam, *Race and Reality* (Washington, 1967); Wesley Critz George, *The Biology of the Race Problem* (no imprint, 1962); Nathaniel Weyl, *The Negro in American Civilization* (Washington, 1962); W. D. Workman, *The Case for the South* (New York, 1960); and James Jackson Kilpatrick, *The Southern Case for School Segregation* (New York, 1962).

Among secondary works which treat the history of segregation and anti-Negro racism, C. Vann Woodward's *Strange Career of Jim Crow* (2d ed., rev., New York, 1966) is preeminent. The ideas of segregation and white supremacy are treated in Guion Griffis Johnson, "The Ideology of White Supremacy, 1876-1910," *Essays in Southern History,* Fletcher Green, ed. (Chapel Hill, 1949), pp. 124-56; James W. Vander Zanden, "The Ideology of White Supremacy," *Journal of the History of Ideas,* Vol. XX (June-September, 1959), pp. 385-402; Rayford W. Logan, *The Betrayal of the Negro* (New York, 1965); I. A. Newby, *Jim Crow's Defense: Anti-Negro Thought in America, 1900-1930* (Baton Rouge, 1965); Newby, *Challenge to the Court: Social Scientists and the Defense of Segregation, 1954-1966* (Baton Rouge, 1967); and Thomas F. Gossett, *Race, The History of an Idea in America* (Dallas, 1963).